LIZZIE

The Letters of Elizabeth Chester Fisk, 1864 - 1893

What do you think of my writing a book on Montana, its peculiarities, &c. ? One might easily gather information, facts and statistics for such a work, which would prove quite interesting.

February 29, 1869

Edited by

Rex C. Myers

Mountain Press Publishing Company

1989

Library of Congress Cataloging-in-Publication Data

Fisk, Elizabeth Chester, b.   1846.
    Lizzie: the letters of Elizabeth Chester Fisk, 1864-1893 / edited by
Rex C. Myers.
      p.   cm.
    ISBN 0-87842-226-9
    1. Fisk, Elizabeth Chester, b. 1846—Correspondence. 2. Women
pioneers—Montana—Correspondence. 3. Pioneers—Montana—
Correspondence. 4. Frontier and pioneer life—Montana.
5. Montana—Social life and customs. I. Myers, Rex C. II. Title
F731.F53   1988   88-39998
978.6'02'0924—dc19   CIP

To

"My dear Mother"

Contents

Vernon Center, Connecticut, home of our Grandparents, Isaac and Azuba Chester, 1875.

Editor's Introduction

Diaries provide immediate, personal observations on contemporary life and events. Autobiographies offer expanded human insights, tempered by reflection. Between the two lie letters. Their composition is sufficiently removed from the occurrences of a previous day or week to provide time for reflection, and on a page or two of stationery is ample room for elaboration. Yet in letters, save those composed intentionally for public consumption, intimate feelings, insights and emotions find form.

Manuscript Collection No. 31 at the Montana Historical Society contains a series of 610 letters by Elizabeth Chester Fisk (she preferred to be known as Lizzie) which reveal the insights, the emotions and the feelings of a pioneer. Their pages reflect the immediacy and hustle of a crude mining camp, the pragmatism of social and political interaction, the civilizing influence of religion and imported silks. In total, two portraits emerge: The first, of a Connecticut-born woman who came West with her husband, raised a family, and settled a frontier; the second, of a community spawned in placer gold along Last Chance Gulch and matured through the collective actions of its citizens.

Lizzie was born February 18, 1846, in East Haddam, a small community along the Connecticut River. During the Civil War, her father, Isaac, took his wife Azuba, and daughters Lizzie and Fannie, to north-central Tolland County, Connecticut, near Vernon, where he engaged in subsistence farming. Under her parents' firm Republican and Presbyterian guidance, Lizzie completed school in 1863 and became a teacher.

1

By chance, she began corresponding with a twenty-seven year old officer in the Union Army during the fall of 1864. They carried on a courtship by mail for two and a half years before she became Mrs. Robert E. Fisk in the spring of 1867. Robert took his bride to Montana, a territory not much older than their acquaintance; to Helena, more particularly -- a bustling, primitive mining camp established in 1864 on Last Chance Gulch.

Along with several other Republicans, Robert Fisk began the Helena *Herald* in 1866, and for thirty-six years its pages recorded the events of territory and town alike. Likewise, Lizzie chronicled the life of her family and community in frequent letters to her mother and sister in Connecticut. She recorded her trip to Montana on a Missouri River steamboat, overland trips by stagecoach or railroad, and community change. She served not only as a reporter, but also as a critic of and a participant in social changes.

Lizzie and Robert had six children -- Grace, Robbie, Clarke, Asa, and the twins, Florence and Jamie -- central topics in many letters after 1869. Raising children in Helena's boisterous mining atmosphere frustrated Lizzie on several occasions, ran counter to some of her New England upbringing, and took most of her days. Yet the former Yankee schoolteacher took time to focus on the world outside her home. She read an impressive list of periodicals and novels, participated in church and social groups, and wrote letters -- detailed letters. These letters reflected her personal interests, recording all the while such occurrences as the mining camp fires which ravaged Helena, Vigilante mobs that meted out justice with a rope, and the political frustrations of Territorial Republicans amid a predominantly Democratic populace.

More than once Lizzie toyed with the idea of writing a book about life in Montana. These letters are her book. They are Lizzie Fisk's record of herself, of her family, of Helena, Montana; and in a very real sense, they are the story of frontier America. The editing process is simply one of condensation on one hand and elaboration on the other.

Transcribed, the 610 letters Elizabeth Chester Fisk wrote between 1864 and 1893 comprise 3000 pages of typescript. What appears in this volume is, therefore, an abbreviation. Observations on the author's style and the editor's technique will facilitate an understanding of what follows.

Lizzie blessed future historians not only with her insights, but also with near perfect spelling and legible handwriting. If she questioned the spelling of a name or word, she noted it in the text of her letter and such notes are included. Where her spelling was in error, the editor resorted to the conventional use of *sic* in brackets. In the few instances where her handwriting was indistinguishable, what appears to be the appropriate word or phrase has been inserted, also in brackets.

Punctuation and paragraph structure used in letters after March 16, 1865, are, with few exceptions, Lizzie's. Prior to that date, Lizzie used little punctuation and no paragraphs in her letters. When Robert suggested she do so, Lizzie complied and the style continued throughout the remainder of her correspondence with Robert as well as with letters written to her mother and sister. Ellipses, signifying edited or omitted material, are in all cases, the editor's. In a final note on Lizzie's style, she underlined occasionally for emphasis. Where this appeared in original letters, it has been retained.

The great majority of Lizzie's letters bear a date, salutation and signature. Where these have been added by the editor, they appear in brackets. Similarly, in the editing process letters have been combined, in some instances, when a proximity in date and subject matter made it possible. To note such transitions, the dates of subsequent letters have been included in brackets. Where Lizzie continued one letter for several days, the different dates or such notations as "Monday afternoon" appear as they would normally.

Each chapter is prefaced with an editorial note on the period. For the reader unfamiliar with Montana's and Helena's history, this will provide some background. Changes in the Fisk family circumstances are also covered in these introductory segments. Where large gaps in time or dramatic changes have occurred between letters, parenthetical notes are inserted, alerting the reader to these events. Within the text of the letters themselves, editorial notes are added in two ways. For brief items, such as first names of individuals, brackets are once again employed. When more elaborate comments are necessary, footnotes provide the required information.

Editing also encompasses more than solitary effort. I am indebted to many people, each important for their unique contribution. Somewhere toward the top of the list, an editor needs to thank his subject — in this case Lizzie Fisk — and the members of her family who preserved the correspondence and photographs, finally donating them to the Montana Historical Society in 1952 and 1977, respectively.

Jeffrey Cunniff, a former archivist at the Historical Society, truly began this project when he brought these letters to my attention during the fall of 1975. Since that time, others at the Society provided assistance, particularly Lory Morrow, who helped glean the Photo Archives; Harriet Meloy, former Librarian who provided encouragement; Brian Cockhill who helped with additional digging into the Fisk Family Papers; plus Bill Lang and Dave Walter who read the manuscript adding their support and expertise.

Understanding frontier medicine, often a topic in Lizzie's letters, became easier through the assistance of Dr. Reginald Goodwin, Helena, and Dr. Charles Eyer of the University of Montana School of Pharmacy, Missoula. Understanding my editing notes proved equally challenging. Thanks to LaNora Brown and Clarice Koby, both formerly at Western Montana College, and Ruby Enevoldsen, South Dakota State University, who typed successive drafts of the manuscript. Vivian Paladin, Helena, understood my enthusiasm for the work, read the manuscript, and helped along the way. The faculty and staff at WMC and SDSU also added encouragement and support. And to reach final book form, an editor needs editing. I appreciate the efforts of Dave Alt, Dave Flaccus and the Mountain Press staff.

Two of Lizzie's grandchildren contributed invaluably to this work. Florence's daughter, Elizabeth White Dittmar, Redlands, California, shared memories of her grandmother. Irene Fisk Blowers, one of Clarke's children, now living in Berkeley, added not only valuable information on family activities after 1893, but also spent many hours of her own time and provided excellent photographs. Most illustrations which accompany these letters are ones Mrs. Blowers graciously donated to the Montana Historical Society to complement her grandmother's letters. After editing the letters and talking with Mrs. Blowers, it is possible to feel like a member of the Fisk family; indeed, she made me welcome.

My own family played a large part in bringing this book to fruition. My wife and children, responding to frequent mentions of Lizzie, think of her as a friend. My parents assisted and encouraged beyond measure. The dedication has a personal meaning.

In the end, however, two people share prime responsibility for what follows: Lizzie and myself. The credit for what is here belongs to her; shortcomings for what is left out are mine. It is my hope and belief that this is the kind of book on Montana she could have written; filled with the information, facts, statistics, and peculiarities she found so interesting.

Brookings, South Dakota   Rex C. Myers
March, 1989

Elizabeth Chester Fisk, early 1860s —Montana Historical Society

Lizzie and Robert — 1864-1867

You must know I have the honor to be
a Yankee school-ma'am.

(Nov. 18, 1864)

Members of the Vernon, Connecticut Patriotic Society
completed several blankets and quilts during the summer
of 1864. These they forwarded to the U. S. Sanitary Commission which in turn distributed them to Union troops
engaged in the Civil War. Secreted in one quilt was a note
from a sixteen-year-old Fannie Chester. The slip of paper
contained the names of Fannie and her two-year-old
cousin Lissie Corbin, plus a list of Patriotic Society members who had helped sew the quilt.

Captain Robert Emmett Fisk, 132nd New York Volunteer Infantry, on duty with Union forces in North Carolina, received the special quilt. Born in Pierpont, Ohio, on
August 9, 1837, Robert was the third of six brothers: John
H., James Liberty, Robert E., Daniel Willard, Van
Hayden, and Andrew Jackson. The family lived variously
in Ohio, New York, and Indiana. By the time Robert
reached 20, he had joined his brother James on the staff of
the Lafeyette, Indiana, *Daily Courier*, where he performed
a variety of duties. Robert moved to New York City in
1861, became a staunch Republican and worked on a
newspaper briefly before enlisting in the New York Volunteer Infantry.

Captain Fisk replied to Fannie Chester's note with a
letter addressed to her and the members of the Vernon

group. Too embarrassed to reply, Fannie sought help from her eighteen-year-old sister Elizabeth. Lizzie Chester was a school teacher in South Windsor, Connecticut, living with her parents Isaac and Azuba Clarke Chester and her only sister Fannie. Isaac Chester was born April 25, 1813, in East Haddam, Connecticut. Throughout the Civil War he farmed near Vernon and championed abolitionist Republican politics. During the administration of President U.S. Grant, Isaac entered government service as a federal revenue collector in the Vernon area; a position he held until his retirement in the late 1870's. Azuba Chester, also a Connecticut native, was ten years her husband's junior. The Chester's were firm Congregationalists.

Lizzie's reply, on Fannie's behalf, began a correspondence that lasted until the Civil War ended in 1865. In July of that year, Robert received his discharge and traveled to Vernon to visit his correspondent. July 21st Robert E. Fisk and Elizabeth Chester became engaged. He left shortly thereafter for Minnesota where he wanted to join brother James's expedition for the Montana gold fields. He promised to marry Lizzie on his return.

The interim between engagement and wedding proved longer than either Robert or Lizzie anticipated. The 1865 Fisk Expedition from Minnesota to Montana failed to take shape, and Robert spent the winter of 1865-1866 in the employ of the Burlington, Iowa, *Hawk Eye*. Robert joined James's expedition to Montana in 1866, settling in Helena. An excellent account of this trip and Robert's actions during 1865 and 1866 may be found in Helena McCann White's *Ho! for the Gold Fields* (Minnesota Historical Society, 1966).

During the intervening time, Lizzie continued teaching. When Robert reached Helena in early September of 1866, he sought work in the newspaper business. With the financial backing of other Montana Republicans, Robert formed the *Helena Herald* on November 15, 1866, and

8

served as its editor. Before spring, he secured a partial interest in the newspaper. Among his first duties was a trip east to secure new presses, paper for the coming year, plus subscriptions and advertisements from St. Louis or Chicago businessmen anxious to secure a portion of the Montana trade. Most important, to Lizzie's way of thinking, Robert traveled to Vernon, intent on marrying his Yankee school ma'am.

Elizabeth Chester and Robert Fisk married on March 21, 1867 in Vernon, Connecticut. They honeymooned in New York City where Robert bought new presses and newsprint for the *Helena Herald*. He and Elizabeth enjoyed the theater and other city amusements during their stay. April 13th they left New York for the long trip to Montana. Hereafter, Lizzie addressed her letters to Fannie and her mother — with the exception of a limited few she sent Robert when he was away on business.

The history of Montana and Lizzie's new home in Helena was almost as new as her relationship with Robert. A gold rush to the placer mines of the region began in 1862 with the first major strike at Bannack. The following year Virginia City and Alder Gulch rose to importance. Population, prosperity and politics combined in the spring of 1864 to create a new territory out of the eastern segment of Idaho — Montana became a reality.

That summer, four discouraged prospectors tried their luck on a small stream adjacent to the Prickly Pear Valley, not far from the Missouri River. They struck pay dirt and Last Chance Gulch boomed. In October, miners gathered to select a fitting name for the infant camp which hugged the twisting stream. Men from an earlier Fisk expedition decided Helena — after Helena, Minnesota — would do just fine. They changed the pronunciation, however, from the traditional Hel-e-na to Hel-ena.

In short order Helena became a prosperous mining camp, supported by a wealth of silver and gold which flowed from the surrounding region. More important, it gradually emerged as Montana's business and financial center. For a decade the political seat of the territory rested at Virginia City, but the economic and social center of Montana was Helena.

Missouri River steamboats brought much of Montana's population and most of her economic goods from 1864 to 1880. Seasonal freighting on the Missouri was furious and short. From the time the mountain thaws swelled the river in April or May until the heat of summer shrank the water volume in July, literally dozens of riverboats made their way to Fort Benton; their holds and decks heaped with the merchandise and manpower for the coming year.

Fort Benton, the head of the Missouri River navigation, served as a funnel through which much of Montana's commerce flowed. At that point the paddlewheel steamers unloaded and wagons or stagecoaches carried the cargoes to their final destinations.

The *Little Rock,* on which Lizzie and Robert traveled, was small compared with other Missouri River steamboats and made only one trip to Fort Benton. It left Omaha on May 16th and arrived at the Montana port at 5:00 p.m., July 14, 1867. According to the Captain's ledger, the trip took 73 1/4 days from St. Louis, with ten days delay for wind and accidents. Included on the manifest were thirty-nine adults — twenty-eight men and eleven women — and ten to twelve children. In addition to the Captain, the crew consisted of eight to ten men. Amid the 125 tons of cargo where the *Helena Herald's* new Gordon Presses and 116 bundles of newsprint — enough to supply the paper for the coming year.

Dangers of Missouri River travel included the possibilities of Indian attack and steamboat wrecks. Snags, rocks, sandbars, and treacherous currents awaited all steamers, and it took skillful navigation to make the 2000 mile trip from St. Louis without incident. River travel also had its more sublime moments. Lizzie's letters captured the full scope of the adventure.

Oak Posts, Among the Pines,
near New Berne, N.C.
September 18, 1864

Miss Fannie Chester:

This is to show that I am the recipient, through the U.S. Sanitary Commission of the Patchwork bed cover or quilt, which you had a hand in constructing.

I am deeply sensible of the obligation I am under to you and your fair companions for this your contribution to my comfort . . . . I am proud to testify to the many sterling virtues of New England women: endowed, generally, with rarest gifts of face and form, and educated in head and heart to adorn the loftiest sphere of the sex, the women of New England stand preeminent in the estimation of their countrymen as the truest sweethearts, the best wives, and most perfect mothers in the land.

I should be much please to hear that this note reached you in safety . . . .

R. Emmett Fisk

Vernon, Oct. 3rd, 1864

Capt. R.E. Fisk,

A few days since, I had the pleasure of receiving two letters written by you addressed to my sister, Miss Fannie Chester, and Lissie C. Corbin. The former being at present busily engaged in school duties and the latter having reached the very mature age of (to use her own words) "two old last July." I have been deputed to answer the said communications . . . .

[Nov. 18th, 1864]

Often we at home are urged to write to our friends in the army, to cheer them in their loneliness, and to atone, in some measure, for the hardships they undergo for us. Again we are warned against a correspondence of this kind, and told that our letters are made subject of ridicule, but after carefully considering the pros and cons I have, as you doubtless perceive, ventured to write again.

For two weeks past I have been engaged in school, for you must know I have the honor to be a Yankee school-ma'am. Imagine me then surrounded by forty children? ranging in age from five to seventeen and possessing characters and acquirements as greatly varied as is this

possessing characters and acquirements as greatly varied as is this
November weather. . . .

[March 16th, 1865]

I invite you now to enter my home and glance at its inmates. Father
busy with his pen, Mother with book and knitting, Fannie dividing her
attention between work, book and pet kitten. (Anna Dickinson by
name). Miss puss will not have occasion to be jealous of either book or
work I fancy, as she receives more notice than both. She is a pretty pet,
but like many another pretty thing spoiled by being petted. Kitty's
mistress believes in "moral suasion" training — [I] presume she never
read something in an old book about "sparing the rod" — therefore if kit
steps inside the pantry door, forbidden ground for her soft little paws,
Fannie takes her up gently, and tells her how naughty it is to do so, and
treats her to a nice bit, for puss has not even been taught that it is more
honorable "to eat the bread of carefulness than of idleness." I have
ventured to suggest that it might be well to try [a] snapper of "legal
suasion" on this whip of Fannie's but the idea was not well received . . .

The glad news of victory comes to us almost daily and in imagination
we view the end of the great struggle . . . . <u>No more slavery</u>. We are a
free people in name only no longer. Is it not grand and glorious to live
in an age like the present, to be a spectator of the wonderful changes,
the rapid growth, the development, the triumph of truth in our land. . . .

Will you allow the school ma'am "to tender her sympathy" for you in
your arduous duties with the wish . . . to learn that you have passed
safely through the contest.

Your friend,
Lizzie Chester

[Victory did, in fact, come during the spring of 1865. On
Palm Sunday, General Robert E. Lee surrendered to
General U.S. Grant at Appomattox Court House. The
campaign in North Carolina concluded shortly thereafter.
In early July Robert Fisk traveled to New York where he
received his discharge. His next stop: Vernon and a visit
with the Yankee school ma'am who had been his faithful
correspondent. July 21st, he proposed and Lizzie accepted.
The marriage would wait, however, until 1867 by which
time Robert established himself in Montana. The correspondence continued.]

Captain R.E. Fisk, 132nd New York Infantry, Co. G.
——Montana Historical Society

Vernon, July 1st, 1866

My dear Robert;

It is such a joy to be able to hear from you . . . . [T]hese messages from your camps along the way, these pen pictures not less than those produced by the art of the photographer, are so pleasing to me . . . .

I rejoice in the prosperity of your undertaking thus far. But Robert, I do sometimes wish that <u>Montana</u> had never been heard of. I know how great and noble it is, to aid in extending civilization and all its privileges and advantages; I rejoice that you have the spirit and enterprise necessary to do this. I would despise a man who could rest satisfied to sit down and fold his hands in comparative ease, while all the wide world is open before him, while there is so much to be done to make mankind wiser and better. But when we come to the sacrifice of those we hold most dear, the thought of a long separation from them, causes us to forget all, save our own selfish pleasure . . . .

[After establishing himself in business as the editor of the Republican *Helena Herald,* Robert left his brother in charge of the paper and traveled East. Among his purposes was the long-awaited marriage.]

[Feb. 16, 1867]

. . . [L]ast night when father came for me at the close of school, he said to me when I was seated in the wagon and our faces were turned homeward, "Capt. Fisk has left Helena (his brother is editor for a few months) and we may soon hope to see him. . . ."

Would you like to know how father obtained his information? That brother of yours sent me a paper, and such an <u>editorial</u>[1] If you have seen the paper you can fancy that the "Connecticut lass" is pleased to have her folly in sending photographs of "inconveniences" published to all Montana, and the world at large. <u>Perhaps</u> I will never forgive him. . .

But you ask me can I "be ready and willing to accompany you to the mountains" should you deem it best for me so to do, on your return. In reply I would say, I will be both ready and willing to go wherever you think best. I love you with my whole heart, and I trust entirely to you to say when it shall be wise and best for me to become your wife. I would not hasten the day, yet it would be a grievous disappointment to bid you farewell for another long absence.

And do not fear, my Robert, that I would not cheerfully undergo any trials or privations which might be encountered. You know I have never

14

never been used to hardship, but I have been used to meet and over-
come difficulties . . . I hope so soon to see you . . . .

Lizzie Chester

Southern Hotel
St. Louis, Mo.
Apr. 19th, '67

To the dear ones at home,

[H]ere we are comfortably established for a week or more at the
Southern Hotel. We have a parlor and bedroom on the second floor, as
good as the house affords, and it will compare favorably with any hotel I
have visited. . . .

This morning we went out and purchased carpeting for two rooms,
thirty-six yards. It is a beautiful pattern, brown and green the colors, a
three ply at $2.25 per yard. Carpets cost no more here than in Hartford.
We have window shades, too, drab and green with green cord and
tassels, and oil cloth for stove, brown and green.

We purchased also a good hair mattress for $50, pillows, two pairs.
These all are to be placed on the steamer *Viola Belle* which leaves here
tomorrow. All the freight except the Gordon Press is already on the
boat. She is the only side wheeler steamer now "in port" and will
probably get through to Benton as soon as some of them which have
already left. . . .

I saw in the hold of the *Viola Belle* the furniture of a young lady who
has gone from this place to marry Mr. [Theodore H.] Kleinsmith, [sic]
cashier of the First National Bank at Helena. She has already gone up
the river. Col. [Wilbur F.] Sanders and family have gone to Omaha. Mr.
[A.G.] Clark and Mr. [Samuel T.] Hauser of Helena are at the same
Hotel with us. We go up to take the boat to Omaha.

When we reached St. Louis we came directly into summer. The
peach trees are in bloom, and other fruit trees will be out in a few days.
The air is soft and balmy as in June. I walked out today with only my
scarlet shawl about my shoulders and even as I write I wipe the
perspiration from my face. . . .

Lizzie C. Fisk

[After securing materials for the Helena Herald and
furnishings for their future household, Robert and Lizzie
traveled by rail to Council Bluffs. There they assembled
their freight and waited for a Missouri River steamboat
bound for Montana.]

Sidewheels moored at the levee in St. Louis. —Montana Historical Society

Council Bluffs, Iowa
May 13th, 1867

My dear Mother:

. . . Our steamer has not yet come up . . . and it is possible that we may take some other boat should one pass the *Viola,* and enable us to transfer our private baggage and stores. With regard to the dangers of the way, do not I pray you entertain the slightest fears on that point. Since we have been here, an account is published of the massacre of the crew and passengers of the steamer *Miner* by the Indians. As the story goes, the men went on shore to cut wood, the Indians surrounded them, cut off their retreat, etc. No one here believes a word of the story . . . This report is only a miserable canard, started, as some people declare, by the [Union] Pacific R. R. Co. I would not have spoken of this, only the account may reach you, and I do not wish you to be alarmed by it. Robert would never take me, or allow me to go where the least danger threatened. . . .

Still, many of our frontier men predict serious trouble later in the season. It is their opinion that so soon as the grass is grown, the various hostile tribes will sweep everything before them on the stage route, unless our government sends out a sufficient force to keep them in check, and this it will not do. A gentleman in the interior of this state told me that five thousand soldiers had been sent out to the territories this spring. "But," said he, "They are mere boys, and not fit for war, and peculiarly unfitted to fight savages. If only the men who dwell in our frontier towns might be armed and organized they would fight to some purpose. They are not only acquainted with modes of Indian warfare, but they would be fighting for their homes."

And with the assurance that we are well and happy and always loving you and thinking of you, I write adieu.

Lizzie C. Fisk

Steamer Little Rock[2]
May 17th, 1867

To the dear Ones at Home;

We left Omaha early yesterday morning, and after taking on Robert's freight, came slowly up the river . . . You would like to make the acquaintance of my traveling companions, would you not?

In the first stateroom on the right, entering at the rear of the cabin is Capt. [John S.] Doyle with his wife and daughter. The Captain is a fine gentlemanly man who maintains most excellent discipline on his

17

boat; allows no drinking, or profanity among his men, and last, but a very important item, understands navigating this most miserable of all rivers. Mrs. Doyle is a lively little lady, very kind and pleasant. Their daughter is about twelve years of age, the leader in all the sports of the children.

In the stateroom No. Two are Capt. and Mrs. Fisk. I would never have believed that one could be made comfortable in such a mite of a place. We have two berths, a wide one below, and narrower above. Under our bed are two traveling bags, boxes, boots, shoes, washbowl and pitchers. Outside our <u>couch</u> there remains a space of six feet long and about three in width. There are two doors, one opening upon the outer deck, the other in the cabin. When we are both in our room, and the doors closed it would seem impossible to get out. But it is fully demonstrated that the thing can be done; indeed I think our quarters grow more spacious every day, perhaps because one becomes accustomed to them. We have driven some nails, and by using the upper berth for a shelf, find room to store away many things. We have tarried long enough in this stateroom. Next is that of Mrs. A.S. Hall of Ft. Wayne, Ind. who is going with three children to join her husband at Virginia City . . . .

Adjoining her room is the pantry, and beyond the gentlemen's quarters. I have not yet made their acquaintance.

On the opposite side of the cabin are Mr. and Mrs. [C.A.] Prouty, who are going out to Virginia City to locate on a ranch. They are eastern people with whom I am only slightly acquainted. Then come Mrs. [Jerome] Norris and her son, a little boy of seven years, from Boston, Mass. Their destination is Viriginia City. Occupying the same room is Mrs. [Jacob] Smith, just think of it!. . . .

Then comes a woman from Alabama [Mrs. Mary A. Starley], a poor white of the South, I fancy, with two little boys — badly behaved children as one need to see. An elderly lady [Mrs. D. Hatcher] is on the top shelf here, whose home is in Montana, but who has been east to consult physicians, being affected with goitre. Her neck is not only painful, but it impedes her breathing. These comprise all the ladies with the exception of the wife of one of the pilots who has three children.

Among the gentlemen passengers are two musicians one of whom plays the violin, the other the guitar. At evenings when the boat is still, we have music, and sometimes dancing. The day is given to sewing, knitting, reading, making tatting, & c. We rise quite early in the morning which necessitates an after dinner nap. The ladies are very industrious, and at the same time lively.

The children have school a little while in the morning, after which they amuse themselves with games, running and romping. All the little girls have their dollies; today they have all been delighted by some

18

whistles which a gentleman made of willow procured on the bank when the boat stopped to wood. This is one of our chief excitements. We watch the men as they tie the steamer; throw out their plank and running quickly up the bank either take wood from the piles already prepared, or failing to find these set to work among the immense quantities of driftwood which line the banks for a long distance on one side [of] the river, varying, as the channel changes, to the opposite shore. . . .

[May 24th, 1867]

Until today we have passed homes of the frontier settlers, but now they have given place to Indian villages. . . . Here, first and foremost, stands a tall chief, his straight, black hair falling upon his shoulders, and wrapped about him a buffalo robe. As he raises his arms to salute the passing boat we find that unlike many another he has some clothing besides his robe, and all his dress, made much like civilized people's, is heavily ornamented with beads, and in addition he wears a string of these about his neck. In these last particulars he only imitates or is imitated by a Broadway belle; the only difference being that his wampum is far finer and handsomer than that of his fair eastern disciple. By his side we see an Indian trader, making a fortune, we suppose, by his association with the dusky aborigines of the country, but becoming constantly more and more degraded, and in many cases taking a wife from among the squaws of the tribe with whom he is associated.

The women of the group on which we are looking, oh, how gaunt and worn and weary they look! Their clothing, so poor and scanty, a mere petticoat, and a shawl or blanket about their shoulders. "The noble red man of the west" are only myth, and the beautiful Indian maids are equally shadowy and unheard of in this country.

Many of the families have comfortable dwelling houses, glass in the windows, with doors and chimneys, but one look at the faces of the inmates of these dwellings is sufficient to convince one of the miseries and discomforts of barbarism. . . .

[May 26th, 1867]

We stopped early yesterday morning at Ft. Randall [present-day Pickstown, SD] and at about eight o'clock at Cedar Island. While new cams were put in the wheels, we ladies had the nicest ramble in the woods. We gathered flowers, we walked about through the underbrush or fallen trees and exalted in our freedom.

The gentlemen took their rifles and shot at a mark, or brought down game from the trees; or the more quiet hung their feet and fish-lines over the bank of the river and waited for a bite. A number of fine fish rewarded their patient waiting. . . .

19

We have everything that is good to eat. Fresh and corned beef and pork, ham, tripe, liver, vegetables, and canned fruits. Capt. Doyle has purchased beaves [sic] or mutton and sometimes both at several towns along the way. Should the supply of provisions fail, which is not at all probable, we have private stores, crackers and biscuit, canned meats and fruits.

Robert and myself amuse ourselves evenings by reading, or playing dominoes; nearly all the other people play cards instead.

*[Friday morning,
June 1st, '67]*

We reached [Fort Sully south of today's Pierre, SD] on Thursday morning. Anticipating a salute from its guns, our cannon was loaded and preparations made to return the compliment; the ladies being admonished not to be alarmed. But our preparations were needless since no salute came. We remained at the landing only a few minutes to mail letters. The soldiers who thronged the bank refused to take these to their office unless rewarded by a bottle of whiskey. This the Captain of our steamer refused to give them; but when the officers came down from the fort the difficulty was quickly settled and the soldiers ordered to their quarters forthwith.

We passed and were again passed by three steamers on Thursday, playing "bo peep" with them, as one or another of the little fleet stopped to wood; but at last we came out ahead and left them in the distance. Yesterday morning we overtook three other boats, and traveled in company with them during the day. . . .

[Tuesday P.M., June 4]

Early on Monday morning Capt. Doyle came rushing into the cabin and shouting something to the men (we were all seated at breakfast); I could only distinguish these words, "Take the guns." Our men were out wooding and my first thought was that they had been attacked by Indians.

But some one shouted "Buffalo" another "Antelope" and a third "Elk" and nearly every man on the steamer ran on shore to join in the chase. One of the animals which proved to be Antelope escaped but the others attempted to swim the river. Our yawl was lowered and the exciting chase began. Every stroke of the oars brought the men nearer their game and when at last they came alongside and raised the poor frightened beast in the yawl, a shout went up from all the watching crowd on the shore . . . The meat when roasted resembled beef. It has however a flavor not found in the latter meat. . . .

Every day is making nearer and dearer these friends who form a part of our little world on the *Litte Rock*. We make morning calls and afternoon visits, and enjoy evening promenades on the upper deck. . . .

With ever so much love to each and all, yours

Lizzie C. Fisk

June 10th, 1867

My dear Mother,

. . . . Last Saturday was a day filled with excitement. First and foremost, our steamer stopped to wood, and according to custom our first relief corps were sent out on picket. Espying a number of antelope running through a defile of the mountains, five shots were fired. The mate immediately, supposing an attack had been made by Indians, ordered the crew on board the steamer, the signal was given recalling pickets and soon the rope would have been cut and our steamer out in the river. Fortunately, a true statement of facts was made and the fears of our people dissipated . . . . For myself, I am happy to state that I was calm and self possessing even though my cheeks may have blanched and my heart sent up one swift prayer to God for Robert, who I knew was on shore. . . .

But the closing episode of the day was saddest of all. One of our deck hands [John P. Valtsin, actually a passenger] lost his footing and fell in the river and being unable to swim, was drowned before help could reach him. He was a Frenchman who had traveled all over the world . . . . Every exertion was made to save him and we each and every one grieved to go on and leave the body which will probably never be recovered. The nature of the river is such that a body lost in its waters is immediately covered with sand and no trace of it can ever again be found. . . .

Tuesday Eve. [June 11]

This morning . . . had an accession to our number of three Indians who came down from Berthold [a fort at the mouth of the Little Missouri River] in a . . . tub canoe made of buffalo hides. Their object was to ride back on the steamer, procure something to eat, and do a little begging for themselves and families.

Robert and myself were standing just outside our stateroom door when one of these braves came around and shaking hands with Robert pointed to me saying, "Squaw." "Yes" was the reply. He then took hold of his pantaloons and raised his long forefinger to tell us he had but one pair. Robert told him much the same manner that he had only the same number.

21

"Big Injun" then asked where we were going and hinted in very gentle terms that he would like one of my dresses for his squaw. Just then the breakfast bell rang and we left our brave; but he was not at all bashful, and, entering the ladies' cabin he seated himself complacently in our midst, having first shaken hands with each person present. He then proceeded to state by means of signs his wants and wishes for himself, squaw and papoose. The ladies talked of making a trade with him but on reaching the Fort it was not concluded.

Long before we reached Berthold the Indians large and small came to meet us, and running along the bank they snatched eagerly at the bits of meat and hard bread which were thrown to them. I wish my eastern friends might have seen these savages, their faces painted deepest red, their wild eyes gleaming and the long hair streaming over their shoulders. They wore little clothing, except blankets and many of the children were entirely naked. They rolled and tumbled and pushed each other about, and displayed all the savageness and ferocity of beasts. . . .

Berthold is situated on a high bluff overhanging the river and, projecting far into the water. In addition to the fortifications and traders' houses are the huts of three thousand Indians of the tribes Ree, Mandan, and Gros Ventres. These huts are circular in form and consist of a framework of logs and saplings bound together and covered with dirt. The fire is built in the center and the smoke escapes through an opening in the roof. The interior is divided into different apartments by robes or blankets. . . .

Monday Eve. [June 17]

We have passed the most northern point of our journey [near present-day Williston, ND] and our course is now almost due west, the river is very crooked and current swift and strong . . . This country is ever new. The bluffs for the last thousand miles show a vein of coal, occasionally lost to sight and then again cropping out distinctly. Many of the hills which here rise in sharp abrupt peaks are streaked with cinnabar. There is not a doubt but that precious metals will one day be discovered through all this region. On the summit of the loftiest of these hills are the petrified bones of fishes and marine animals. Some terrible upheaval must have cast these little mountains up, and the sun and wind and rain have carved their sides in every conceivable form and shape.

Good bye — We are at [Fort] Union tomorrow.

Lizzie

Steamer Little Rock
June 20th, 1867

My dear Fannie:

. . . We met with an accident yesterday which proved quite a serious one for us. The escape pipe burst and before the injury could be repaired thirty bundles of Robert's paper which was stored in the hold were wet and very seriously damaged. We had it brought to the upper deck and yesterday afternoon and the greater part of today has been spent in opening, spreading and drying. . . . The outside quires of every bundle are of no use except for wrapping paper while those on the inside are very much injured not only by the hot water and steam which penetrated to the innermost parts of the compactly arranged bundles, but by the dirt, and stains from the brown wrappers which have given to all the paper a gilt edge. We are, however, glad that no more serious injury was done.

Since [June 8] . . . nothing has "gone right" as [Captain Doyle] expressed it; . . . we have but half a crew owing to illness, wounds, and bruises and you can imagine that the working of our steamer is not the most smooth and agreeable. The ladies too, with very few exceptions, have had some little misunderstandings and there are jealousies and cliques. Do not fear that I am involved. . . .

The chapter of accidents yesterday consists of attempting to cross from one bend to another on dry land and in consequence striking the bank with such force as to endanger the lives of all on board the boat. . . The shock was truly terrible. Our dinner table was moved two feet toward the stern and soup, meats, and vegetables were mingled indiscriminately. Every piece of china or glassware on the pantry shelves was thrown to the floor, bottles of catsup, pepper sauce, were broken and their contents spattered over the crockery. . . But we live in hope. . . Once past Fort Buford . . . we seem to have entered upon the last stages of our long voyage. Only seven hundred and fifty miles more will bring us to Benton. . . .

Sunday Morn. [June 30]

On Friday evening we passed Milk River . . . We passengers are almost led to conclude that our officers being paid by the month and having no hope of making another trip are determined to prolong this voyage till its utmost limit. Our potatoes are nearly gone, our white sugar <u>ditto</u>, and we had no milk for our coffee this morning.

Everyone is "down on" the Captain of the boat. All the preparations for our journey were of the cheapest kind, even a sufficient number of men were not hired. Owing to the want of care much of the freight consisting in great measure of groceries have been allowed to spoil. Robert finds his paper in a most miserable condition. It has become

The steamer Helena *calls at the Milk River Landing, 1880.*

mildewed and musty and the mice have nibbled paper and string . . .
More than two thirds of the bundles have to be opened and rechecked.
He can collect damages of the steamer as other parties are doing but
three times the cost of the papers would not restore this to him or
render it possible to purchase more in the east before another year
comes around. The want is more than the worth of it . . . .

Sunday Morn. July 7

We have suffered much during the last ten days from the intense
heat. I have never experienced such dry, burning air as we get here on
this little tug. But Benton was never so near as today and the showers
of two or three evenings previous have cooled the air and we are living
in hope. . . .

With much love I remain Yours
Lizzie C. Fisk

Helena, Montana, July [21], 1867

My dear Mother:

Our steamer reached Fort Benton on the afternoon of Sunday last.
We came into port amid the firing of cannon and shouts of the people
assembled on shore. We had been long and anxiously expected and
many fears entertained concerning our safety. Our passengers were
more delighted than words can express to know that their long "Misery"
was at an end. . . .

Fort Benton was a pleasanter town than I expected to see and wore
an air of life and animation. The ox and mule teams awaited their loads
of freight were drawn up on the river banks, while further back, on the
broad plain on which the town is built, were hundreds of cattle and
mules feeding on the rich grass. . . . Our route lay over the most
beautiful prairie, a level natural highway. At evening we came to Sun
River where we were delayed four hours waiting for the coach from
Helena. . . .While our coach stopped to change horses, I stretched myself
out on the seat and took a little nap, awoke thoroughly chilled and
entering the little cabin warmed myself by the fire and drank a cup of
hot tea. Soon we came to the crossing of the Dearborn, and forded the
stream and rushed on our way as before. The rain was falling fast and
at every steep hill our gentleman passengers (I was the only lady) were
obliged to unload and walk up the mountain side. They were wet to the
skin and a more dismal looking party could not have been found.

But amid it all we kept up good spirits and laughed and joked. . . .At
three o'clock in the afternoon we entered Helena and received a warm
welcome from our friends here. We were in truth almost frozen and
although warmly dressed our clothing proved insufficient. We felt at

25

home at once in brother Jim's neat little cottage, and after a warm bath and a change of clothing we felt refreshed. Brother Jackey [Andrew Jackson or A.J. Fisk] came up from the office to welcome us, with Mr. [Charles R. Stuart] the foreman. Yesterday Brother Van [Hayden Fisk] came in from the mines, and is spending a few days with us. . . .

I am much pleased with this country, and can already think of it as home. We passed through Prickly Pear Canyon on our way from Benton. Here is some of the most beautiful scenery in the world. The loftiest mountains, their peaks covered with snow, towered above our heads, while in the valley were the most lovely wild flowers in bloom — roses . . . blue bells, and many other of whose names I cannot tell. The mountains rise all about our home, their sides sometimes covered with pine and cedar and again only with the green grass. The snow still lingers on the tallest peaks and the wind is cold and wintery which sweeps down from their sides. . . .

---

[1]James Fisk's editorial of January 17, 1867 read in part: "We are not entirely satisfied that . . . press, & c. is the only object of his mission, for we know of a certain Connecticut lass way down there, who has of late been throwing out some very broad hints, and forwarding in this direction some quaint photographs depicting the 'inconveniences' of bachelor life. . . ."

[2]An expanded article on Lizzie's riverboat trip appeared in Rex C. Myers (ed.) "To The Dear Ones At Home: Elizabeth Fisk's Missouri River Trip, 1867," *Montana, The Magazine of Western History*, XXXIII, 3 (Summer, 1982).

Helena — 1867 - 1869

I like the place much; it is not like home, but there is a wide field for usefulness here, and, entering upon the work earnestly and prayerfully, One need never be lonely or disheartened.

(July 31, 1867)

Helena held challenges and excitement for Lizzie and Robert. Several Fisk brothers followed the lead of James L. and settled in the bustling community. James's home at the corner of Rodney and 7th Avenue became the family headquarters and "home" for Lizzie and Robert during their first year in Montana. Also residing permanently in the home were Lydia Ann (Goodie) Fisk, James's wife, and their two and one half year old daughter Dell. Lizzie spent the first year longing for a home of her own, but pitching in to assist with family duties which included feeding other Fisk brothers as they dropped in from time to time.

Robert and the *Helena Herald* faced severe challenges during 1867 and 1868. These involved questions of legal control as well as editorial politics. James W. Whitlatch, reportedly one of Montana's first millionaires, owned the Whitlatch Union Mine south of Helena, nine separate ore processing mills in the vicinity, and a major portion of the *Helena Herald*. During the fall of 1867, he decided to assert himself in the newspaper's management. When he attempted to cut wages, most *Herald* typesetters quit in protest — one of Montana's first labor disputes. Whitlatch also suggested the paper cease publication during the winter months to save money.

27

Main Street, Helena, Montana Territory, 1866. L to R: Wells Fargo & Co., Pioneer Cheap John. Savage & Ottinger, photographers —Montana Historical Society

Frustrated at the meddling, Robert, in partnership with another minority owner — Charles R. Stuart — decided to buy out Whitlach's interest. They agreed to a contract with the mining magnate in which they would pay off the sale price over a period of two years. Whitlatch held the note for the remainder due, but relinquished all editorial and policy control.

As spokesmen for Montana Republicanism, Fisk and Stuart advocated Negro suffrage in the Territory. The issue proved unpopular — "radical" — among some Republicans and Montana's Democratic majority. Although guaranteed by law, such suffrage in Montana became difficult to implement in many locales. Assuming a more moderate stance, the *Herald* simply dropped its insistence on voting rights for blacks. Before long a schism formed in Montana's Republican party. George Pinney represented the radical segment, while Fisk and Stuart (if for no other reason than practicality) espoused more moderate views. At stake and at issue was the confrontation in Washington between President Andrew Johnson and Congress — the victor in either instance enjoying the spoils of political appointments and patronage.

To ensure economic and advertising success as well as to mend political fences, in Washington, D. C., Robert Fisk decided to travel east during the winter of 1867-1868. Stuart stayed in Helena and managed the *Herald*. Lizzie also remained in Montana.

Robert's efforts proved successful. Charlie Stuart's management did not. He yielded to the temptations of liquor and was unable to walk a compromising line among Montana's feuding political factions. Robert returned hurriedly in May of 1868 to quiet the waters Stuart had roiled. The situation continued to deteriorate, exacerbated by Fisk's strong attack on Helena Postmaster John Potter — guilty of bribery and corruption, according to *Herald* editorials.

Tempers flared. George M. Pinney bought the *Montana Post* in Virginia City and moved it to Helena to combat the *Herald's* influences. Gunfire erupted and one of Fisk's supporters was killed. Pinney's and Potter's animosity culminated in September of 1868 when they purchased the *Herald* notes James Whitlatch still held and attempted to force Fisk and Stuart out of business. The effort proved unsuccessful. By the end of 1868, Robert Fisk and Charles Stuart emerged in full control of the finances and editorial policy of the *Helena Herald*.

Lizzie alternately worried and rejoiced, sharing the business and drama with her mother and sister by letter. On occasion she worked in the *Herald's* job department, sometimes helping with book binding. She had her own concerns as well. Shortly after her arrival in Helena, Lizzie contracted dysentery. Its severity confined her to bed for over five weeks and accompanying high fever resulted in the loss of most of her hair. As her health returned, so did her participation in Helena's social life, including church, theater and calling.

Throughout her first year in Helena, a constant theme of Lizzie's letters is the desire for her own home. In June of 1868 she realized the dream when Robert rented a place not far from the James Fisk residence. Delighted, Lizzie unpacked all the furnishings brought up by riverboat a year earlier.

During Robert's eastern business trip from late December of 1867 to May of 1868, Lizzie enjoyed a level of independence uncommon for middle or upper class women on the frontier.[1] Sometimes she traveled alone, sometimes in the company of one of the Fisk brothers, and sometimes with bachelor physician William M. Bullard. Public schools did not exist in Helena during this period, so Lizzie called on her previous expertise, and tutored several children in the James Fisk home. She charged $1 per week for her services.

Politics and a variety of economic and social issues captured Lizzie's attention as well. She longed for a railroad and reliable transportation in Montana. Missouri River steamboats operated seasonally at best. The Union Pacific and Central Pacific railroads built toward an eventual junction at Promontory Point, Utah, during the spring of 1869, but even then a long, bumpy stage ride awaited anyone desiring to travel east.

Montanans — Lizzie among them — also expressed concern over hostile Indian activities in the region. Blackfeet, Sioux, Cheyenne and other plains tribes constantly harassed parties traveling to and from the Montana gold fields. Residents long maintained that the U.S. Army did not take sufficient action to prevent Indian depredations in the territory. Lizzie joined the chorus for more troops and more forts.

During the fall of 1868, Lizzie became pregnant. After the resolution of the *Helena Herald's* affairs in Montana, Robert, decided to make another trip east. Once more he wanted to secure supplies and advertising for the 1869 mining season. The 1869 Presidential elections also placed a new man in the White House — Ulysses S. Grant. As a former officer under Grant, Fisk sought to take political advantage of the opportunity.

Lizzie wanted to have her first baby in Connecticut. Robert promised before his 1867 trip that Lizzie could accompany him if he went again. Now she insisted. New Year's Day, 1869, Robert and Lizzie boarded the Wells Fargo stage in Helena and traveled south, ultimately to board the Union Pacific in Wyoming, bound for the east coast.

The Fisk brothers: Andrew J., Van H., standing; Daniel W., James L., John H., Robert E., seated left to right. —Montana Historical Society

[My dear Mother:]

I must tell you something of Helena. . . . The streets, with few exceptions, are narrow and crooked while ditches of mining purposes cross and recross many of them. The buildings are mostly of wood, an occasional stone block relieving the monotony. But there is through all the streets an air of life and bustle which is pleasing to witness and which gives promise of future good for the country. . .

[Helena, July 31st, '67]

[D]uring all [of last week] we have had only one eastern mail and that one brought no letters for me. Wells, Fargo & Co. are great swindlers and great monopolists. With their immense capital on which to perform business, they "buy out" every opposition line of coaches or mail wagons, and oblige every one to wait for them. They regularly bring through passengers and express matter for which they will be paid, but having contracted for the mails, and being sure of their pay at any and all hazards, they toss the bags containing all those letters, books, and papers which are reminders of the continued affection of absent friends into any convenient gulch or defile of the mountains. . .

On Sunday we attend church, The Methodist North, Rev. Mr. [A.M.] Hough. The building is of logs put up in the rudest manner, rough wooden benches and a pine pulpit, yet I am sure the worship which went up from the grateful hearts there assembled was not less sincere than that arising from many a nobler edifice. . . . But in good time we shall have a prettier place of worship, and, indeed, the foundations for a new church have this week been laid.

Men who never enter God's house contribute liberally of their means toward the object. The congregation was small yet I think many more would attend if there were a better church. . . .

My first impressions of Helena have been generally confirmed. I like the place much; it is not like home, but there is a wide field of useful-ness here, and, entering upon the work earnestly and prayerfully one need never be lonely or disheartened. There is room here for every one to win a name and an influence that shall be widespread and shall ever be for good on all those around. For these, if for no other reason, I like the place. . . .

Lizzie

Helena, Aug. 7th, 1867

My dear Mother,

On Saturday. . . Gen. [Alfred H.] Terry and brother dined with us. It was an intensely hot day, but we had a nice dinner, roast beef, spring chickens, new potatoes, and other early vegetables, pie, peaches, cake, and wine, comprising the bill of fare.

I wanted much to see Gen. Terry, not only for his . . . fame, but for the reason (in this far away country far more potent) that he came from Connecticut. As we were both so far from home, we considered ourselves old neighbors and greatly enjoyed the meeting.

The Gen. is a tall, slender man in manner most pleasing, yet dignified. He has a fair complexion, piercing blue eyes, and a straight nose, while his cheeks are round and full . . . . He quite came up to my ideal of a commander in our army and I thought of those words applied to Washington, "First in war, first in peace" and one might almost add "first in the hearts of his countrymen." . . .

We have also entertained Martin Beem (the young man who is correspondent of the *Herald* under the cognomen <u>Ben. E. Ficial</u>), and who is now Adgt. Gen. of the Territory under Gov. [Green Clay] Smith; and Col. [W.F.] Sanders whom we met east, the Republican nominee for Congress; and Dr. [James] Gibson, P.M. [Postmaster] at Virginia [City].

The present is an interesting and exciting time. The fall campaign is already begun . . . . Gov. Smith . . . has been spending a few days in Helena, and every evening has been thoroughly intoxicated and in this condition has attempted to address groups of the citizens, chiefly Democrats, who were assembled to know the illustrious man. He has thoroughly disgusted all loyal men and his departure from the country would be considered for the country's good. . . .

[Aug. 22nd, 1867]

Robert is working so very hard, he never comes home before one o'clock at night, and last night . . . it was five when he left his office. This labor is of course very wearing, and today he [is] almost sick, and I am discouraged. They can get no help in typesetting that is worth having; the errors in the late papers are most disheartening to an editor. . . .

[Goodie] Fisk . . . has no <u>goaheadativeness</u>, if I may use the word. She hires all her washing and ironing, has a colored man who cooks all the meats and vegetables, scrubs the floors, washes all the dishes, she has bought the greater part of her bread, pies and cakes since I came here, and has scarcely found time to do her mending. She does no sweeping or dusting except her own room either. Do you candidly believe there is need of giving all one's time to one child [Dell], a healthy one at that?. . .

O, I do so long to get a house of my own. I want to make some night shirts for Robert, my green dress is untouched, sheets and pillow cases unmade. Besides I wore my black alpaca on the steamer, and as it is soiled, it must be cleaned and repaired. . . .

34

I have attended church only twice, one half day each time, since our arrival in Helena. . . . Neither Capt. [James] or Goodie [Fisk] have been inside of a church since they left Minnesota and both are church members. Their religion is of that kind which believes in a good dinner on Sunday, and on that day Goodie reads a Psalm. How uncharitable I am . . . What can be expected of a community at large, when those who profess to be governed by good motives thus live . . . .

Saturday afternoon

The Herald Printing Office is this day removed from the dirty, old, establishment on Bridge St., to new and commodious rooms [at the corner of Jackson and] Broadway. The papers, daily, tri-weekly and weekly, are in a flourishing condition, have a large circulation and, with the next issue of each, are to be enlarged. I trust you receive the weekly paper regularly,. Jackey [A.J. Fisk] mails them to you. I will also send you an occasional daily. . . .

> With love to all.
> L.C.F.

Please send me recipes for cakes, cookies, &c., &c. Also one for cologne, and your hair preparation.

Helena, Sept. 2nd/67

My dear Fannie:

[F]or two weeks I have been enjoying your most troublesome complaint, diarrhea. . . . [M]edicine seemed to have no effect unless I entirely abstained from food. . . . But I am well again now, which is to be chiefly attributed to the exercise I have taken, both out and in doors, not less than to food better adapted to an invalid. . . .

I made bread on Saturday and would like to send you a piece; it is very nice. Fabricated some pie, too, after my most approved style and sent some to the office hoping to get [an editorial] puff, but it doth not appear. Can you credit my words when I tell you that, in this country where milk well watered is one dollar per gallon, and eggs one dollar and a half per dozen, I made cream pies. And today, I have been guilty of the further extravagance of cooking for supper a spring chicken for which I paid only $1.25 in [gold] dust. Such is the fact, and not a bone is left to tell the tail, but we had visitors at tea, Stuart and Jackey, and we don't have chickens every day.

Today has been election, the day so long [and] anxiously awaited and on which events so much depends. We can as yet have no idea of the result, but can only hope that our territory will have no such delegate in Congress as James M. Cavanaugh.[2]

The day has been one of much interest yet in this city it passed off very quietly. Had it not been for an event which occurred late in the day we might have been proud of the manner in which our citizens conducted themselves. The negroes of course voted and this raised some disaffection among the rebels. Late in the afternoon an Irishman shot a negro without the slightest provocation and for no reason at all, unless it were the color of his skin. The colored man cannot live it is thought, and the son of Erin will without doubt be hung, with little delay and not much of a trial.[3] The Vigilantes keep things in order here, and I truly believe there is less of crime in this city than in any town east, of the same number of inhabitants. This I consider high praise, remembering the elements of which society is in a great measure composed. . . .

What would you think of a town with no grass, no trees, no flowers, only dust and stone in the streets and yards. Such is our town. . . . Nothing grows here without irrigation. This however might easily be accomplished since ditches run through all the principal streets. I intended making a garden another year. Send along the seeds please, both flower and vegetable, as soon as you gather them and they will be in season. . . .

Your sister
Lizzie

Helena, Oct. 15th, 1867

My dear Fannie:

[J]ust now they are having quite a serious trouble in the office. Mr. Whitlatch, by virtue of his money invested in the concern, thought he would <u>run it</u>, and, going into the office one day, told the men that he could not any longer pay the prices he had been paying. This after they, the printers, had met a week before and voluntarily reduced the price of composition from $1.15 to $1.00 per thousand. . . . Every man in the office except one left.

Mr. Stuart and [Robert] went on with the paper, working night and day for a time, but at last they gave up and we have had no paper in several days. What the result will be we cannot tell. . . . [Whitlatch] has offered to sell out for twenty thousand dollars, ten thousand to be paid down, the remainder made up in two years. . . .

[Oct. 22, '67]

[T]oday Fisk and Stuart are proprietors of the Herald. They had to pay [Whitlatch] a portion of the money down, which sum has been advanced in part by their friends in the city. The remainder is to be paid in periods of one and two years. . . . Mr. W. has shown himself a very small man in his dealings, although he was more liberal toward

36

the last. He is rendering himself very unpopular here, has scarcely a friend in the city, and people are beginning to lose confidence in his reputed wealth. He is evidently "hard up" for money at the present time. . . .

Friday morn [Oct. 25, 1867]

We have two excitements in Helena at the present time, the revival of the paper and — the theatre. R. has a free pass for himself and lady but he lends it to his brother every evening. Col. & Goodie have attended several times. I think that was one motive which induced them to attend church, having been seen several times at this place of entertainment. . . .

Lizzie C. Fisk

Helena, M.T.
Dec. 15th, 1867

My dear Mother:

We are having unusually mild weather and considerable rain. The streets are exceedingly muddy at present, the frost leaving the ground as in the spring and could one only hear the birds we might fancy that delightful season had come. I have not seen or heard a bird since I came here save two or three crows, huge creatures, which were loudly cawing down in the valley. They reminded me of the two famous

> "old crows sat on a tree
> As black as ever crows should be.". . . .

I wish you could take a walk through the streets of our town and witness the bustle and stir, the rush of business. Contrary to the usual custom there is much more being done in the way of trade than during the summer. There are six quartz mills in the immediate vicinity of Helena crushing out the precious metal where there was only one last winter. River navigation having closed, few people are leaving the country and money is consequently spent here. Merchants and other business men are advertising largely and furnishing the office a good run of job work. . . .

We have much to be thankful for. Main Street and indeed Broadway are at present Sloughs of Despond and the individual who ventures forth must be possessed of an immense amount of hardihood. The first mentioned of these highways runs north and south through the gulch, is very low and uneven, and has sidewalks, of wood. . . . Up and down, down and up, trailing one's clean skirts through the mud is far from pleasant. Why the city was ever placed in this low land, while all around rise the beautiful hills affording much finer sites, would ever be a mystery were it not for the one magic word, gold.

37

A sentence from Virgil's <u>Aeneid</u> here recurs to mind: the Latin would not interest you, the translation may, "O' accursed love of gold! to what will you not lead human hearts?" . . .

[Dec. 28th, 1867]

About two weeks [ago] the subject [of a trip east] came up for discussion and it was thought best [for Rob] to visit the cities of Omaha, St. Louis and Chicago to solicit advertising for the paper. . . . I did not attempt to dissuade him from his purpose or offer any objections, for I knew that on the results of the coming year all future success depends. It was a great disappointment to us both that I could not accompany my husband. Want of funds alone prevented. . . .

Having once decided it was best to go, no time was to be lost for the deep snows of winter were coming on. R. left us this morning at six o'clock. Unless detained by storms he will reach Omaha in twelve days. . . . He will be absent four, five and possibly six months, during which time he will come east to New York and Washington and of course will visit you. It was hard for him to leave me here, [and] all the life and joy seem gone out of my life, and my ambition has suddenly vanished.

Christmas passed away as such days are wont to do. . . . I received a fur collar from Rob, and from Mr. Stuart twenty-five dollars to be invested in a gift. He said "I never made a lady a present and did not know what to get. You can please yourself in the selection." I intend to buy books, some standard works. No other gifts would please me so much. . . .

No paper was issued on that day and Rob was home for a few hours. In the evening we called on Misses [T.H.] Kleinschmidt and [George M.] Pinney's, returning visits paid me when I was ill — a long time to wait, yet this was the first opportunity presented for leaving home. . . . Mrs. Pinney. . . is a perfect lady, and proves a most excellent mother to her husband's children who seem to love him dearly. It is a course of much wonder how a girl, educated as she has been (she was a star singer, . . .) can prove so good a wife and mother. She urged me to come and see her often during the winter. . . . The Kleinsmiths [sic] are pleasant people, but somewhat dutchy.[4]

We have little or no snow as yet, and on Christmas day it was not cold enough for skating. Montana is not so terrible a country.

With love to all, Your daughter.

L.C. Fisk

38

Rob darling:

I am trying to be obedient and sometimes I fancy the house would stagnate, then blue, were it not for me. The Col. is still absent and Goodie bewailing the circumstances. Dan is fussy and annoys Goodie by interference in household matters. Mr. Stuart is in deep sorrow.

Your Elsie tries to be a minister of mercy to each and every one. I pinch people's ears, pull their noses, steal hats and overcoats, compelling the owners thereof to remain with me. I read aloud to the groups, start games for their amusement, and try to make them all happier. . . .

I wish my dear husband were here with his genial sunny temper, to cheer the sorrowing ones, to make all glad by his presence. I want your strong arms about me, my darling, lest I faint under the burdens of the day. I have been strong till now and tried to lighten other's labors, now if I could rest my head on your shoulder and feel your soft kiss on my face I could indeed rest.

God bless and keep you in the arms of his love.

L.C.F.

Helena, Jan. 19th, 1868

My dear Mother:

I wish you might be present at some gathering of our citizens, the better class of young men in particular. I have been often struck with the fine manly countenances, the vigorous, well-knit forms. We have no idlers, no shirkers, among us. Every one comes here with an object in view, and labors hard to accomplish his purpose. All are earnest self-reliant, courageous, hopeful, prepared for ill fortune if come it must, yet hoping for good. We have the best men of the east, those whose living will be of greatest good to the country. How many far away mothers, sisters and lovers have given their best loved ones to build up new towns and cities among the auriferous mountains. . . .

Every mother who has sons or daughters here should be proud to tell of her interest in the country, for each one, often unconsciously, is helping to shape the destinies of our common land. . . . I want to stay here, to identify myself so closely with this land that I cannot live elsewhere. Here is elbow-room, here earnest Christian men and women are needed. The east is full, why are not more seeking wider fields of labor. . . .

[February 1st, 1868]

The services of last Sabbath are still fresh in my mind. The sermon in the morning was one of a series of discourses on the parable of the sower. . . . The text was "The prudent man foreseeth the evil and hideth himself.". . . It was a <u>loud</u> discourse, and at its conclusion a prayer meeting was held, and special petitions for an outpouring of the Holy Spirit were offered. . . . In the midst of all this our good dog Pilot, who accompanies us to church, became too warm and set up a combined groan, cough and howl. You can imagine the effect upon my keen susceptibilities. I could not laugh. I was shocked at my own wickedness for desiring to do so. Oh mother, why did I ever have so keen a sense of the ludicrous!. . . .

Among the events of the past week I must tell you of a visit at Mrs. Durgan's,[5] the good widow down on the ranch. Wednesday evening, bright and beautiful, saw us a party of fourteen snugly stowed away in a "big sleigh" drawn by four horses, on the road leading from town to "the valley." A nice ride, and fine supper, sweet music and merry games were the order of the evening. These old fashioned reunions are always pleasant.

I have enjoyed one other sleighride, with Dr. [William] Bullard who had business calling him to Unionville and wished my company. I don't know but I shall set the gossips talking, but as this is the first and only time I have ridden with him I do not greatly fear. Divorces are fashionable here, and it is a common remark that a man in the mountains cannot keep his wife. The community is worse than our old eastern towns; people are on the lookout for scandal. At least this is what those more experienced than I tell me. My own observation furnishes no proof of the facts. . . .

I believe I am not growing old so fast. . . . My health was never better, I am "plump as a partridge" the boys tell me and "rosy as a milk maid." But my golden locks once abundant are diminishing rapidly. My head is now covered with a soft <u>down</u>, fine and curly. I shall do well by and by. I would like another braid of hair. Will you match it by your own? I wish a <u>long</u> one this time. . . .

[Feb. 9th, 1868]

We were honored (?) during the last week by an evening's visit with the Gov. of Montana, Hon. Green Clay Smith. . . . Dr. [I.E.] Baker and daughter . . .were invited to meet with us. Col. Howie being an intimate friend of Col. Fisk must needs be included and having a previous engagement with Mr. [S.H.] Bohm, one of our leading bankers, brought him here also. Dr. Bullard and Gov. Smith with Mr. [T.N.] Chemidlin completed the party. After an hour's pleasant chat, refreshments, cake and apples, wine and cider, were served. Goodie and I fought against the wine, taking a most valiant stand in favor of cold water, but without success. How can men put poison in their neighbor's lips? Our <u>worthy</u> Gov. could drink neither of these beverages but took brandy by himself.

At tea time I had announced my intention of laying siege to Mr. Bohm, being sure he must have <u>piles of gold</u> and when by the merest chance I found myself seated near him I endeavored to improve the time to the best of my ability. He is an interesting little German Jew, his wife and four daughters now abiding in the fatherland. I found him quite entertaining and I think made him my friend as he was before my husband's. . .

Society here is one constant whirl of gaiety. Dancing schools, parties are the only life our would-be young ladies enjoy. The idea of rendering assistance to a weary jaded mother never seems to enter the mind of one of these butterflies. Will they make helpmates for men in their own stratum in life — I often asked myself, and then thank God that I had so excellent a mother. An earnest woman wields a vast amount of influence in this community as in any other, but it seems here to be so much more needed and widely felt. . . .

L.C. Fisk

Helena, Feby. 22nd / '68

My dear Fannie:

[On] my birthday, Jackey devoted a portion of the day to me taking me for a pleasant walk early in the morning. We visited the photographic gallery and were transferred to glass and paper. . . . After returning home we practised shooting at a mark. With a few more lessons I shall make an excellent shot, they tell me. The Indians have again commenced their depredations in some portions of our territory and I might want to shoot them or somebody else.

Montanans are (to use a Montana phrase) <u>down</u> on Gens. [William T.] Sherman and Alfred Terry for their course with regard to Indian difficulties. They represent that there is no danger of Indian hostilities and memorialize Congress not to make appropriations defraying the expenses incurred in support of our territorial militia. Simply because they were not scalped and our peaceful homes laid waste. . . there is <u>no danger.</u>

I doubt if eastern philanthropists will ever awake to a realizing sense of the nature of the foe we of the west must deal with. Indian character must be seen and studied for one's self. Words can't convey any proper idea of the cunning cruelty, treachery and meanness in general of "poor In.". . .

[Feb. 29th, 1868]

We shall be rich people by and by. I hear men about town wishing they "owned half the *Herald* Office." Last autumn when "the boys" took possession of the establishment all old croakers were prophesying a

41

"HERALD OFFICE" THE PROPERTY OF FISK BRO'S.
HELENA.

Herald Office —Montana Historical Society

grand "smash up." They, and every one else in fact, begin to open wide their eyes, and think they may have been mistaken. The worst part of winter is passed and not a debt contracted. . . .

Everybody is at the theatre this evening except Jackey and I. We two staid, sober elderly people are home taking care of the baby and keeping the house from running away. To use Jackey's words "We don't go much on these vanities."

This remark opens a new field for remarks — our mountain vocabulary. I never dreamed that so many slang words and expressions could exist. A person who chances to be hung or shot is "out of luck." If you dislike a man, "You don't go a cent on him." If you agree to any contract, "you bet I'll do it." A man out of funds is "dead broke." A person who disappoints your expectations is "a bilk." There are many other phrases equally amusing.

What do you think of my writing a book on Montana, its peculiarities, &c.? One might easily gather information, facts and statistics for such a work, which would prove quite interesting. . . .

[F]or the first time since coming here I must acknowledge that I am homesick. I am weary and would rest. Three or four months must elapse ere I can see my dear Rob again. Will the time never end?. . . .

May god bless and keep you all. . . .

L.C. Fisk

[During the spring of 1868, the political and economic situation of the *Helena Herald* began to deteriorate. Central in the controversy was a schism within the Republican Party between moderate and radical factions which complicated existing Republican/Democratic conflict. Charles Stuart — managing the *Herald* in Fisk's absence — was unable to ameliorate the situation. As a result, Republican George M. Pinney purchased part ownership in the *Montana Post*, removing it from Virginia City to Helena, in direct competition with the *Herald*.[6] To make matters worse, Stuart developed an affinity for liquor. This did not facilitate his business or political maneuvering. As crisis approached, Robert Fisk cut short his eastern trip and returned to Helena on May 6th to take charge of affairs.]

My dear sister Fannie:

[You] are advised of the state of affairs politically in our mountain town. . . . The removal of the Post (Virginia) to Helena will probably injure us somewhat. We are to have three dailies in town the coming summer. Of these *The Herald* and *Gazette* have laid down their weapons of war and banded together to fight, run out, and annihilate The *Post*. With the latter institution managed by one so unpopular as Mr. Pinney there can be little doubt of the results. . . .

Radicalism in Montana is not the wisest course. Only by dropping this part of political faith [Negro suffrage] and striking broader ground can a paper be sustained or a party formed which shall win ascendancy over the Missouri-rebel Price-army faction of the territory.[7] I am free to confess that I do not like to appear to go back on one principle enunciated in last autumn's campaign. Such a proceeding was equally distasteful to Rob, and nothing save the belief that only in this way could the desired end be attained could have induced him to drop radicalism. People in Montana were forced to adopt the same conclusion which was borne home to their sister states in the east with regard to Negro Suffrage: — the time for its successful promulgation has not yet arrived.

[Mch 27th / 68]

My birthday gift came to me yesterday, the sweetest little canary. He has been singing all the day and now hangs on the nail just above my head quietly sleeping, with "his head under his wing, poor thing." I shall take so much comfort with my little pet. I have named him Will. . .

My only fear is that the mice will devour him bodily at night. We are overrun with these little pests. They run races across my pillow at night till I rise and shake them off or light a candle. I expect to waken some morning and find my nose or ears eaten off. I shall feed the little pests with arsenic tonight and then perhaps they will not like me so much. . .

Your[s] ever,
L.C. Fisk

Helena, Apr. 5th, 1868

My dear Mother:

I hope that Rob will be able on his return to buy out Mr. Stuart's interest in the office. . . The circumstances transpiring during the past month have convinced us all that Charlie is an unsafe partner, particularly, to be left with the sole charge of business.

The attentions paid him as Rob's partner seem to have spoiled him
. . . If I needed any reminder of the peril of touching <u>one drop</u> of ardent
spirits the lesson has been brought home to me . . . during the three last
weeks. I cannot understand how any man can be as lost to every
principle of manhood as to [seek] in intoxication relief from sorrow.

Charlie has not been free from the influence of liquor during all that
time, and has made a complete fool of himself, nearly ruining not only
himself, but all those connected with him and that business of which he
is head during Rob's absence. . . .We were compelled to telegraph for
Rob and in three weeks I hope to see him. I don't know if it be best to
laugh or cry when I think of it. . . .

Charlie's "spice" terminated in something as near delirium tremens
as I ever care to witness. He is now quiet, too weak to move. I don't
know but 'tis wicked, but I often think it would be better for him to die.
People might have some charity for him then; and I would rather know
that he was in his grave than liable to so conduct himself again. . . . .

Mr. Smith asked me last evening; "do you like this country?" My
reply was "I do like it. I am perfectly happy and contented here if I can
have my husband with me, and have a home.". . . Contented, happy
wives and mothers are the exception. No one comes here to stay longer
than until their fortunes are made and the idea of building here a
comfortable house and making a pleasant home is not for a moment
cherished, by a majority of our citizens. I tell every one I have come
expecting to remain here. I look upon this "The New Northwest" as my
home and shall try and do all in my power to build up that home, and
make it desirable. . . .

[May 10th, 1868]

The weather since the first of February has been delightful, but far
too pleasant for the best good of the country. There is little snow in the
mountain ranges from which to expect the June rise in the water.
Mining claims in all our gulches are laid over till another spring. There
was never before so much gold on the surface of the ground waiting only
to be "washed out" as in the present season. And water, the one great
want of mining countries, is not. . . . Rain or snow, even in limited
quantities could make this year of 1868 the most prosperous Montana
has ever known. . . .

[May 17, 1868]

During these last few weeks, when it seemed as if there were little
hope of a prosperous season, when the very windows of heaven seemed
closed against us, I could not believe that God would forget us. . . . The
effect on business was terrible. Our merchants with somber, cloudy
faces sat behind their counters waiting for money and customers which

came not. They thought of their heavy freight bills, and looked with a sigh at their empty purses and the big piles of uncollected and uncollectable bills. Now [it is raining and] every one is once more brave, cheerful and hopeful, and Montana is "looking up.". . .

The controversy with Mr. Pinney (he is the man who married the star - not singer, but danseuse, and she has just presented him with a fine boy), was called for. . . . Mr. P., as chairman of the Central Com., attempted to "run" the Republican Party of Montana and shape everything to his own ends. He is anything and everything for the sake of power. Ambition is his god, and he aspired to be the great man of the territory. Failing to control the *Herald* and make it as extremely radical as himself (at the present time) he was angry and made some foolish remark about placing the paper "on probation."

During Mr. Stuart's illness (I try to be charitable) Mr. P. attempted to use him, when under the influence of liquor, to carry out his own ends. Stuart would drink with him, tell him "the quarrel between them was at an end," and at Mr. P.'s request signed some important telegrams for parties in Washington, which were exactly opposed to all his former course and messages to the same senators to whom the telegrams were addressed. We thought everything ruined for a time but prompt action warded off the anticipated evil.

This, then, is Mr. Pinney's character, restless, ambitious, unscrupulous; at one time endorsing Andy Johnson, at another out-radicaling the extremest radicals. . . .

With love untold to all, your daughter,

L.C. Fisk

Helena, May 24th, 1868]

My dear Mother:

. . . I sent you a long letter by Tuesday's mail, but as news has just come to us that the eastward-bound coach was robbed yesterday, near Pleasant Valley [Idaho], I deem it possible that this letter of mine may have been one of those torn up by the desperadoes, and cast to the winds. We seem to be living over again and the early days in the history of our territory when murders, robberies, depredations and lawlessness were on every side and the Vigilantes were engaged in their terrible, awe-inspiring works. These Vigilantes must again organize in every part of our domain and bring miscreants to swift punishment. Mild measures will never do for reckless savages or still more daring white men. . . .

We have experienced showers or heavy rain each day since a week ago last Thursday. . . Every day during the past week in water-proof and over-shoe I have splashed down to the office through the mud to engage in the work now occupying my attention — book binding

[Helena Business Directories]. My labors are nearly at an end; a few more covers pasted on will put the finishing touch to seven hundred and seventy-five books. No small amount of work, I can assure you and the stitching, with awl and mallet, is very hard for the hands and arms. But I persevered and have my reward in looking at the piles of neat pamphlets and the amount of money they represent to the office. . . .

I enjoy being down there so much. It is so quiet and orderly one can think, and to some purpose. One meets, too, so many people, sees so many peculiarities of character, is amused, interested and disgusted, by ignorance, real worth and kindly feeling or downright impudence.

Let me introduce you to some of our visitors. . . . Mr. Stuart enters and seating himself at a table in another part of the room commences his "leader" for today's paper. Creaking boots are heard on the stairs, ... and the door opens to admit Gen. Sol. Meredith, Surveyor General of Montana. . . . He is tall, six feet six, slightly stooping, has a kindly face, with bright blue eyes, iron gray hair and whiskers.

In political life he represents the <u>conservative element</u>. . . .He talks too much, however, and has no time for doing. Talks! He is like a machine which once set in motion glides on forever in one ceaseless round repeating and re-repeating his pet ideas and theories. . . This much I know of Gen. Meredith, whatever his eccentricities: he is an incorruptible man, . . . one of Montana's best officials, a hard-worker with but little remuneration. . . .

Having ventilated his ideas the Gen. withdraws. A few minutes of quiet ensue when in stalks, hat in hand and coat tail flying, Mr. Geo. Pauncefort the eminent actor of the Helena Theatre. At the door he pauses. "Ha! A lady! Shall I enter? Yes!" and he enters. "Good morning, madam. Pardon me for appearing before you in such attire," all uttered in one breath, is his salutation.

His dress let me describe. It seems to be made up of the cast off articles of his theatrical wardrobe. A checked flannel shirt; drab pants covered at intervals with patches of buckskin of every conceivable size and shape, boots reaching to his knees and bespattered with mud; a black and white coat, checked, of the style of some fifteen years ago, a knocked up hat and gauntlets. The reason of this singular style of dress I learn. His engagement with [theatre manager J.S.] Longrishe concluded, he has purchased for himself a good horse a two-wheeled vehicle to which he adds a cover of bright yellow painted cloth. His turnout is most amusing, original and unique, and in this style he proposes to make the trip to California giving readings from Dicken's Christmas Stories along the way. . . .

Mr. Whitlatch, with his <u>owner</u>, Mr. [L.H.] Herschfield[8] appear on the scene. Mr. Stuart has meanwhile gone to dinner, and I am left to do the honors of the Sanctum. Mr. H. in tight fitting spring pants and stylish coat alarms me by his very low bow. They examine my work, and Mr.

W. states that I have "marked all these books." Two scoundrels as I know them to be, I cannot afford much graciousness. . . .

Once more I am left alone for a few minutes, but soon a printer announces "Mr. [Frank] Kenyon" of the Deer Lodge *Independent*. I remember the hard things he has said of Rob and the *Herald*, but one glance at his crutches and useless limb removes all unkindly feelings and I bid him welcome to the Sanctum. We never get on well in talking together, do not seem to have any sympathies and tastes in common, and conversation soon flags. "Frank" is a handsome man despite his broken limb, said to be irresistible with the ladies, but he does not so appear to me. His stay is but short and quiet soon again reigns.

I glance out at the window to refresh my eyes with a view mountainward, and my attention is caught by a huge placard posted on one of the out-buildings. "H.R. Horr, Attorney at Law." This young gentleman was a Capt. of Montana militia, not destitute of brain but exceedingly indolent. He lounges about the office and this practical joke at his expense is a source of much merriment. . . .

I have not much faith in mankind. The world is selfish, supremely selfish, and no part of it more so than. . . . Montana. People coming here, leave behind all the grace and goodness they ever possessed, and live only for money getting, They are true to no principle of right or justice, make friends only to advance their own interests. . . . The temptation is often great to make my home, when I shall gain it, my world, to seek no companionship outside its little circle.

Could I only decide the question -- Shall I, too, selfishly address myself to money getting and ignore the claims of society upon me, or shall my influence be used to bring about a better state of things and beget a little public spirit . I should then with all my heart and soul address myself to the one or the other.

Love untold for all.
L.C. Fisk

Helena, June 7th 1868

My dear Mother:

Let me tell you how greatly I am at present rejoicing and the cause of my delight. Mrs. [C.H.] Ellis, our next door neighbor, has been for some time in feeble health. . . . [S]he suddenly decided to "go home" and, her mind once made up, she sent for me asking advice and assistance in making preparations for departure. This gave us the first chance, and Rob at once rented the house, and made arrangements to buy their cow. At last we have a home, a pleasant one it is too. A log house, clap-boarded and plastered, containing three rooms, a cellar, and an upstairs for a store-room. We have besides the privilege of making one hundred dollars worth of improvements and applying the same toward the rent. . . .

Our cow is the most remarkable cow in Montana. She is a very proper kind of a cow. She walks demurely over the hill to join the remainder of the herds (We have no fenced pastures here but herders in their stead.), feeds all day and comes home at night all by herself, calling for us to let down the bars that she may enter her little door yard. . . . She gives us a pail of milk night and morning. I have not as yet made any butter, and the prospect for supplying the market is not very flattering since we drink the greater part of the lacteal fluid supplied by our cow. . . .

Do you know I am the only bride of last year who has not done her <u>duty</u> shall I say, toward increasing the population of Helena. I never did like to be like every one else. . . .

[July 5th, 1868]

My new home shall come first. . . . The parlor carpet is green with wood colors, the furniture black walnut with green seat cushions for the three chairs, an easy chair to match, and a handsome center table. The curtains for parlor and bedroom are drab, with a light buff tinge, and green bordered. Cords and tassels green.

The oak chamber set, the plainest but handsomest I ever saw, is all of oak. It has none of these gaudy landscapes only carvings and mouldings. The bureau is large, three large drawers, two small ones, a marble top and a mirror attached. The washstand has also three drawers, and let me record the fact while there is time, one of them has nothing in it. Three chairs, cane seat, and a rocker complete the set. . . .

I put down the rag carpet in my bedroom with one breadth of the three ply in front of the bed. The china for the chamber is green hawthorn and is absolutely beautiful, in pale green leaves and flowers contrasting so finely with the clear white. One thing I must mention, the spring mattress is a great luxury and so far as I know the only one in the territory.

The dining room is carpeted with the remainder of the house, with the exception of the passage way on the south, which is covered with matting. Here are table, flower boxes at each window, two chairs and the wicker of the set, and one brought from St. Louis a year ago, the bureau Mr. Ellis made for me and the bird. Over the table a mirror, frame mahogany and gilt. And here we have come to the cupboard and its contents. Only one dish was broken in transmission and that large yellow earthen for baking a chicken pie at Thanksgiving. There were a half dozen yellow pie plates and three deep dishes. One of these was broken.

I have one dozen each of the three sizes of plates, 1 dozen soups, one dozen each tea and coffee cups and saucers, sauce plates, sugar bowls, cream cup, three bowls, four platters, soup tureen and ladles, britania and earthen, sauce boat and ladle, potato dishes covered and uncovered, butter dish, goblets and pitchers. I look around for something else and espy the tea pot in the corner; a very pretty server too, white and gilt band upon black. My silver has all been cleaned and a small part of it in use. . . .

Let me open my kitchen door to which I am proud to invite you or any one else to enter. The floor of rough pine boards has been scrubbed to whiteness (Rob gave me a scolding for this performance, solemnly declaring that floors in general and this one in particular were never intended to be washed), the stove too has been blacked and the greater portion of the accumulated rust removed. This stove, a Charter Oak Extension, is an excellent one, and with the larger boiler at the back and tin heater underneath I have always hot water and a hot dinner without drying should that meal be compelled to wait.

Here are shelves for the milk dishes, a large table and a sink where much of my time is spent.

My first meal cooked in the new house was Thursday's breakfast, [and with] the first baking [of] cake. . . bread and pies, I had excellent success, indeed everything tastes so good and is such a change from Chinese cooking that I eat too much every day. We have breakfast, lunch, and dinner, as it best accommodates Rob. . . . Need I tell you that Rob and myself are most delighted and so domestic. It is a trial to leave our little paradise even for one evening. . . .

Love untold for all.
Lizzie

Helena, July 13th / 68

My dear Mother:

Our home is pleasant, mother, such a little bit of Paradise. . . I would tell you how rich we are in provisions. . . Two barrels of sugar, white and brown, one sack of Java Coffee, two cases of canned fruits and vegetables consisting of peaches, pears, plums, strawberries, pine-apple, tomatoes with oysters and sardines for variety, one kettle of golden syrup. . . .

Our sugar costs us here at the rate of twenty cents [per pound] in greenbacks and our merchants retail it now for about thirty in gold. Other things in the same proportion. Sugar has been selling during the spring for seventy-five cents, gold; at one time there was not a whole sack in town, and as fast as stores arrived they were put carefully away during the night.

The merchants of Helena are a set of monopolists. We have three times as many as we need in the first place and they must resort to such expedients or go down. Some of them deserve it. . . . As a consequence of these insecure business houses, we have a small stock of groceries brought to Montana this year. At the present time potatoes are twelve cents per pound and none to be bought at that or any other price. . . .

I intended in my last letter to tell you something of financial matters connected with the office. The payment last October was made and we entered hopefully on our preparations for meeting the first note due Aug. 20th, 1868. It was the consideration of this seven thousand dollars which chiefly influenced Rob to undertake his journey east. Up to the time of his leaving they made over and above expenses more than two thousand dollars. After he went away they paid expenses. This was all. Nor is this to be wondered at. We had an expensive family numbering anywhere from five to ten members; [James Fisk] returned from Virginia [City] and in less than one week spent all his summer's earnings, Goodie had medicines and doctor's bills.

The only wonder is that the *Herald* lived with such a burden to carry. Van [Hayden Fisk] needed money to keep his mining interest running and who so ready or able as his brother to accommodate him.

All this might have been borne, but Stuart must needs neglect his business and disgust enemies and friends alike by a spree of nearly a month's duration in which he threw away several hundred dollars. The subscriptions fell off, the office ran behind five hundred dollars in one week. . . .

Ere Rob's return matters were looking up a little and it needed only his presence to complete the good work. . . . The freight bills are all paid, $4000 in all, and they have from Mr. Whitlatch, who is again the good friend of yore, an extension of a year on their note at 1 3/4 percent a month in place of 5%, the usual rate.

The payment might have been met with ease had it not been for the large family they must support. And now comes in another item. [James L. Fisk] has a mining interest on American Bar[9] which he and some others consider rich, but without thoroughly inspecting it he has employed thirteen men to put in a ditch. He has no money and no credit and today his bills amounting to some six hundred dollars are presented to Fisk and Stuart for payment. They are responsible for $650 in addition. Rob now says "We can go no further. We must not ruin ourselves to help another." I cannot believe they have right to get in so deep.

Thus for the outgoes. A brighter side let me present. Fisk & Stuart have brought to Montana a stock of printing paper and other material worth twenty-six thousand dollars. Two small notes are still unpaid but they can easily be met when due. Fifty thousand dollars would be no inducement to them to part with their office old & new, and, indeed I do

51

not know as twice that sum would tempt them. We have our fortunes here. Is it wrong to regret that there are so many to share them? . . . .

We are now enjoying beautiful summer weather. . . . But — always that fatal but — I found a bed bug one morning when making my bed and another since. Quicksilver came quickly to the rescue, I pray you. . . . I am sorry the former occupants troubled themselves to leave the seed behind. But won't I slaughter them!. . . .

L.C. Fisk

Helena, Aug. 16th, 1868

My dear Mother:

The early Sabbath morning here is as peaceful and quiet as at home. A solitary milkman or the ice cart are the only sounds that disturbed the morning slumbers of meditation of the residents of Rodney Street. Later in the day the tide of travel from the valley is set in motion.

The farmer harnesses his horses or mules, and with his family comes "to town." A few attended church, but the great majority gossip with their acquaintances, drink poor whiskey, and return home at nightfall, worse than when they came. Sunday is the great day for bringing to us a new revelation of country living.

The miner too, drops pick and shovel, turns the water from his sluice traces, and mounting his faithful pony rushes to Helena to spend his week's "earnings," it may be wisely, but usually is foolishly and wickedly. The faro banks, hurdy-gurdy halls and saloons today reap a rich harvest. It is a good thing, pecuniarily to be the center supply in a mining country, but a sad one morally and religiously. . . .

[Sept. 13 / 86]

Let me tell you how the religious wants and needs of [Helena's] ten thousand people are cared for. The first church established here was of course the Methodist South. The first settlers of any number were rebels. They were ignorant, and the preaching of the minister sent to them, the Rev. Mr. [B.R.] Baxter, was quite good enough. . . . He had a family of twelve or fourteen children, the care of which bound him down to the earth, clipped the wings of his mental and spiritual powers. . . . His congregation was always larger than the M[ethodist] E[piscopal] and combined more wealthy individuals. . . .

[Rev A.M.] Hough was first settled in Viriginia City [as the Methodist minister]. When that place began to go down as Helena built up he thought he would make more money by coming here, and hence we were <u>blessed</u> by his presence for two years. He could not claim that the people did not support him. As Montana had no bishop he drew a

52

bishop's salary and passed the contribution box twice every Sunday. He had three thousand dollars loaned out at five percent per month at the time of his leaving. . . .

My recent letters have made you acquainted with our new pastor, Rev. George Comfort. We have every reason to be thankful that as good a man has been sent thither. His whole heart is in his work. . . . He is most deeply in earnest. The prayer meeting is well attended and a young people's meeting organized. . . .

Mr. Comfort while a good man is very illiterate and his remarks not always in good taste. People receive him kindly and his congregations are larger than of old. . . . He is sustained by eastern societies and asks nothing from Helenaites save their interest and attention.

I think I may safely say that exclusive of the Catholics who have a large and prosperous church, not two hundred people assembled on Sunday to worship God. And where are the thousands who should meet with them? Where were they last Sabbath?

Some fifteen hundred were at the prize fight. Probably five hundred more were present at the two horse races. Another hundred were at the ranches and pleasure resorts about town visiting their friends. Their wives, did they possess any, stayed at home. And many of these were young men who would have scorned such an action in the east. Here they outrage no public moral sentiment. . . .

During the high winds of late prevailing many fears have been expressed concerning the safety of the town. Those who have been for any length of time acquainted with frontier life predict that the coming winter will see our city laid in ashes. We can only hope for the best. . . .

Your loving daughter,
L.C. Fisk

Helena, Sept. 21st [1868]

My dear Mother:

Today I am considerably disturbed by news Rob brought me this morn. . . . [In] Helena during the past week [has been a] U.S. Mail Agent. His avowed purpose was to investigate Postal matters in this city; and many grave charges were preferred against Mr. [John] Potter, P[ost] M[aster]. But a little of the gold which some men prize above honor even, closed his eyes and ears to all wrong doing. The *Herald* made a fearless expose of the matter which highly incensed the P.M. and at the instigations of Mr. Pinney, that most infamous of all scoundrels, the P.M. has bought of Whitlatch, who is closely pressed for money, all the *Herald's* papers. . . .

No harm can possibly result to them, yet it is so vexating to know that the money of which Mr. Potter has defrauded the government is applied to such a purpose. Mr. W[hitlatch] has several times solemnly promised never to allow these papers to leave his hands, but I suppose Pinney over-persuaded him. We would prevail on any man of Mr. W.'s calibre to believe his soul was not his own. . . . But yield to him we never will. . . .

Helena, [Sept. 27 1868]

. . . The sale or transfer of which I told you was completed and Messrs. Pinney & Potter became owners of the *Herald's* obligations. They of course made use of this fact to their own advantage and also refused the interest, then due, claiming both principal and interest. We don't have much law out here and Mr. Pinney is ever "a law unto himself" in cheating his creditors or imposing on honest people. . . .

On Wednesday evening as Rob and Stuart were standing outside the back door talking earnestly concerning the state of affairs, two bullets were sent toward them, one of which passed through Stuart's hat, and the other pierced the house just between them. They were much startled although often warned. . . The neighbors soon collected and the bullets were found but nothing and nobody else. As might be expected the affair created much excitement about town and deep and loud were the threats and curses uttered by our "roughs" who are friendly to the institution.

The occurrence, startling as it may appear, is almost forgotten in consideration of a tragedy of later occurrence. [Former Minnesota governor Samuel W.] Beall, through rendering assistance [in preparing] more important charges against our P.M., has incurred the ill-will of Mr. Pinney who published in the *Post* a most bare and ungentlemanly attack on the old man. Col. Beall is the soul of honor and uprightness and was deeply wounded. He published a card in reply. . . in the *Herald*. This exasperated Mr. P. still more and he came out in two articles still meaner and more cutting.

The Gov. replied not, but called on Mr. P. telling him he must retract, when the latter drew his derringer and ordered him to leave his office. The Gov. appealed to a bystander for the loan of a pistol wishing to fight a duel. He was refused and soon left the place.

On Friday morning [Beall] . . . in some way . . . procured a pistol and paid Mr. P. another call asking him to step into another room. It is claimed by the friends of the latter that the Gov. held a pistol in his hand during the interview, but it seems not very probable that a man holding a pistol cocked should stand still and suffer a revolver to be fired so close to his face as to fill it with powder. . . . One cap snapped, the first shot entered the wall, the second entered the Gov.'s face just below the cheek bone and penetrated to the brain. Gov. Beall fell instantly and continued unconscious till Saturday at eleven A.M. when he died.

That no blame attaches to him we do not claim. But he was an old gray-haired man and, with his nice sense of humor would never have used the weapon he carried save on equal terms. If Mr. P. had stepped from behind the desk where he sheltered himself, placed himself in position and fired at a given signal, the Gov. would have been satisfied. . . .

[T]o think that the gallant veteran of so many battles should fall by the hand of such a villain, that he should leave wife and children to come to Montana only to be murdered seems sad indeed. And Mr. Pinney walks the streets today a free man. . . . the funeral services for Gov. Beall were held today at the Catholic church. An escort of soldiers and sailors. . . attended the body . . . These sad events are of too recent occurrence to permit one to write on other subjects. . . .

With much love for all,
Lizzie

Helena, Oct. 3rd 68

My dear Mother:

The world seems degenerating; or is it only that as one grows older they [sic] learn its way and wickedness better. How long must evil men triumph?. . . Since the *Herald* was established it has fought bad men and evil measures. Shall it now falter, deterred either by fear of the assassin's bullet or the tricks of sharpers who would wrest from its owners their all?. . .

Mr. Pinney has commenced the suit to recover property to the amount of nearly forty thousand dollars, including costs of proceedings. We do not expect that justice will be done. If the new Judge - [Hiram] Knowles - is accessible to bribe our case is certainly already decided. . . .

[Oct. 25th 1868]

Our case came up for trial on Friday evening and was to have been completed last night, but on the occasion of a farewell benefit at the theatre, Mr. Pinney presented not only all his counsel but <u>the judge</u> with tickets and consequently court did not assemble.

Mr. P. has constantly sought delay. He thinks he can manipulate Judge Knowles and, by numerous drinks and theatre tickets, procure a decision in his own favor. . . . I have not much faith in, or respect for, any person or thing. I shall be ready to leave Montana soon for some more congenial sphere. Since the shooting affair, nearly four weeks ago when people began to think we might lose the office, my friends prove only for "fair weather" and although some eight or ten ladies are indebted to me for calls only two have had the courage or have cared to come and see me. . . Those who cared for me only while I sustained my position in society and was the wife of a man successful in business are welcome to find more prosperous friends. . . .

[Nov. 2nd/68]

Glory enough for one day! "We'll beat them fellers yet!!" . . . With pride and honor I record it — Judge Knowles is an honest man — and I must add that my faith in mankind is greatly strengthened and my hopes for the future of our loved territory are far brighter.

There being no theatre or other place of amusement open, "our case" came up for trial on Monday evening last. The great attempt was to prove the *Herald* material decreasing in value daily, and, assuming on the start Fisk & Stuart to be insolvent, it must hence be necessary to appoint a receiver to take charge of said material pending the judgment of the court on the action for foreclosure of mortgage.

The case was tried mainly on affidavits and some of the biggest lies were sworn to be the enemies of the *Herald*. Mr. Whitlatch . . . stated he had been a <u>publisher</u> during nearly two years; that he was well acquainted with the value of printing material; that it constantly deteriorated in value, about one fourth yearly. And I venture to assert that he cannot tell a case of type from an inking form, a shooting stick from a galley. . . .

Judge Knowles took time to consider and read up the case and render his decision only this morning. It was as I have told you, adverse to Mr. Pinney & Co. The foreclosure on [the] mortgage is yet to be tried unless our enemies have abandon[ed] the case as a bad one for them. . .

Following the advice freely tendered by many friends, "to set our house in order and be prepared for any event," many things of value on which there was no mortgage were mysteriously disposed of. Some six or eight thousand dollars worth of type and other material walked off one night last week. No one saw it go but we know it was <u>in the hands of friends </u>and asked no questions. All the presses except the one in daily use have lost some important part. It is worth something to have a few trustworthy friends. . . .

[Nov. 14th 1868]

Since losing his case in Court, Mr. P. has been very anxious to conciliate the successful parties. He finds his newspaper a constant source of expense and fully alive to the fact that two Republican journals cannot live in a town the size of this, his constant effort, failing to break down the *Herald*, is to unite the two. That man even had the impudence to <u>call here</u> to discuss the matter with Rob. That our dear little home should have been thus desecrated! He paid two or three calls

56

R.E. Fisk "Mansion" in Helena, Montana. —Montana Historical Society

at the *Herald* office and made several offers not one of which could reasonably have been accepted, as the controlling interest was to be left in his hands. . . .

With love, untold love, for all the dear ones.

L.C. Fisk

Helena, Nov. 23rd/68

My dear Mother:

Business is dull, provisions of all kinds rapidly increasing in price, flour already fifteen dollars per sack (1/2 bbl) [half barrel or 52.5 quarts dry measure], and a snow storm which we may any day expect, would send it up to thirty dollars. I wonder if it really is a man's duty, when he has a wife of his own, to support the whole family of brothers. . . A little surplus cash would clear away all the doubts and troubles I fancy. . . .

The present mania about town is for building nice houses. Four are going up in our immediate vicinity. . . . Dan Fleury, a noted gambler, also "decorated" our part of town with a handsome house for his mistress, it is supposed. Mrs. [Daniel C.] Corbin, an Irish servant girl in her younger days if we may believe former acquaintances, now aspiring to much style and showy dress is soon to occupy a new house near us. . .

Mrs. [Timothy] Wilcox and Mrs. [Cornelius] Hedges, both Connecticut ladies are also living near me. . . . When last I met Mrs. Wilcox, I introduced the subject of another church than the Methodist. She is a very plain outspoken little woman yet always so cheerful and full of good nature that one cannot take offense at anything she may say. She told me "Mr. Comfort comes in here and calls me 'sister.' I tell him I am not a Methodist, never was, and never will be one.". . .

I have thought of adopting one of three courses. To turn heathen at once instead of allowing the work to be gradual as it is with most Montanians; to attend the Catholic church and perhaps get to be a saint; or to call in a few kindred spirits and hold some kind of religious service every Sunday. . . The third . . . seems the only possible good. . . .

I am knitting socks for Rob from the yarn you sent me. It is so fine, soft and warm. . . .

Your daughter,
L.C. Fisk

[1]Two works by Paula Petrik are excellent for placing Lizzie's life in the context of women and the family on the frontier. "Mothers and Daughters of Eldorado: The Fisk Family of Helena, M.T., 1867-1902," *Montana, the Magazine of Western History,* XXXII, 3 (Summer, 1982) examines Lizzie, her daughter Grace and their relationships with one another as well as Helena society. Petrik's later book, *No Step Backward: Women and Family on the Rocky Mountain Mining Frontier, Helena, Montana, 1865-1900,* (Montana Historical Society Press, 1987) broadens the perspective.

[2]Democrat James M. Cavanaugh defeated Republican Wilbur Fisk Sanders 6,004 to 4,923.

[3]John Leech killed Sammy Hayes. Although Leech was arrested, there is no record of his ever standing trial or being executed by vigilantes. In all probability, he escaped.

[4]Theodore Kleinschmidt organized an active German social club in Helena.

[5]Mrs. Durgan or Durgin came to Montana as a widow in 1862; settled along Ten Mile Creek in the Helena Valley in 1864; and operated a boarding house and truck garden there until her death in 1888. She remarried in 1871 to an Edward Whitcomb. Her house was a popular "resort" during Helena's early years.

[6]Montana's first newspaper, the *Post* began publication as a weekly in Virginia City in August of 1864. The paper moved to Helena in April of 1868 and offered daily competition to the *Herald* and *Democratic Gazette.* This effort failed and the *Post* ceased publication June of the following year.

[7]For a discussion of the Union/Confederate, Republican/Democratic conflict in Montana see Stanley R. Davison and Dale Tash, "Confederate Backwash in Montana Territory," *Montana, the Magazine of Western History* XVII, 4 (October, 1967), pp. 50-58.

[8]L.H. Hershfield and Company, a Helena banking house, helped finance James W. Whitlatch's mining ventures around Helena.

[9]A placer mining area north and east of Helena, along the Missouri River.

Grace Fisk, about 1877. O.C. Bundy, Photographer.
—Montana Historical Society

Baby Grace — 1869-1872

*Her loving little heart compensates for many
a little faults.*

(Aug. 9, 1871)

Grace Chester Fisk was born May 21, 1869 at the home
of Lizzie's parents in Vernon, Connecticut. Robert and
Lizzie did not return to Helena until fall that year. During
their nearly ten months absence, Vernon became Robert's
headquarters, but he made frequent trips to New York
City for business and to Washington, D.C. for politics.

On her return to Helena, Lizzie found the camp mark-
edly changed. An April 28, 1869 fire destroyed most of the
business district and produced property damage in excess
of $50,000. The hasty log and frame structures of the
boom town gave way to the permancence of brick and
stone. Lizzie perceived a change in the community — a
transition from boisterous mining camp to aspiring urban
center.

Fires provided subject matter for several of Lizzie's
letters during subsequent years. In June of 1872 the
Herald's new office burned to the ground— a total loss.
Two months later a larger conflagration once more ravaged Helena's business district creating $140,000 in
losses. Major fires remained a constant threat.

In many ways Helena still bore the frontier mark. A
"Hanging Tree" in Dry Gulch, not many blocks from the
Fisk home, saw periodic use; Joseph Wilson and Arthur L.
Compton among its victims. The pair shot and robbed

61

Missouri Valley rancher George Lenhart the evening of April 27, 1870. Lenhart lived to identify his assailants whom the county sheriff arrested and jailed. The morning of April 30th, a crowd assembled, removed the men, tried and convicted both, then proceeded to hang them — a day Lizzie long remembered.

With her mother and sister, Lizzie shared other Helena excitements. During August and September of 1870, the nineteen-man Washburn-Doane Expedition explored what became Yellowstone National Park. Henry D. Washburn, Montana's Surveyor General, headed the civilian contingent (nine men, including such Helena residents as N.P. Langford and Cornelius Hedges). Lt. Gustavus C. Doane commanded a military escort from Fort Ellis, near Bozeman. The group returned in late September amid much publicity and celebration, but without one of their members. Truman C. Everts, a former Territorial Assessor, became separated from his companions on September 9, near Yellowstone Lake. The expedition tried in vain to locate him. Spurred by the offer of a $600 reward, several parties scoured the region until trappers George A. Pritchett and John Baronett found Everts, near death, on October 16. Publicity stemming from the Washburn-Doane expedition helped secure formation of Yellowstone National Park in 1872. Langford became its first superintendent.

Territorial fairs, church bazaars, and traditional holidays kept Lizzie and Helena busy. In 1870, Robert bought a lot at 319 N. Rodney in Lizzie's name. On the site they had a new home constructed and moved in during September of 1871. Through a variety of additions and modifications, the home served as Lizzie's place of residence during the rest of her life in Montana.

The Robert Fisk home gradually became the Fisk family headquarters in Helena, assuming the function from the James Fisk household. Fisk cousins Mae and Julia joined the Montana family, sometimes staying with James, sometimes with Lizzie.

In her own family, Lizzie shared success and tragedy. Her sister Fannie left Vernon to teach in a Freedmen's Bureau school in Georgia during 1870. Willingly, Lizzie supplied her with magazines and other reading material. Fannie contracted typhoid fever and returned to Vernon where she died on October 19, 1871. Suddenly the distance between family and Helena seemed all the greater to Lizzie because she could not be with her family during this time of sorrow.

Robert's actions continued at a hectic pace. Business and politics took him out of town on several occasions. He had helped secure the appointment of Territorial Governor James M. Ashley in April of 1869. Ashley's uncompromising political views alienated some Montana Republicans (like Wilbur F. Sanders) and most Democrats. Under pressure, President U. S. Grant replaced Ashley with Benjamin Franklin Potts. Fisk opposed the decision and went to Washington in February of 1870 to fight for Ashley's retention. He succeeded only in delaying the appointment until July. Potts proved more moderate and acceptable to most Montanans — Republicans as well as Democrats. Throughout most of Potts' tenure (1870-1883), he and Fisk remained at political loggerheads.[1]

Lizzie and Baby Grace became interested observers of Montana's political activities, particularly the campaigns for Territorial delegate to Congress. They attended public meetings and parades; heard speeches; and even joined Robert for one of his trips east.

In the process of her travels, Lizzie recorded the exigencies of western transportation — dusty, bumpy stagecoaches and hastily constructed railroads. Like all Montanans, she and Robert shared a vital interest in securing one or more railroads for the territory, particularly the transcontinental Northern Pacific (which would connect the territory with Minneapolis and the Pacific Ocean) and a branch line of the Union/Central Pacific, up from Utah. Robert joined a group of Helena businessmen during

September of 1872 in an attempt to interest California financiers in constructing the latter line. This effort proved interesting, but unsuccessful.

Cares of home and motherhood often eclipsed public issues in Lizzie's mind. She worried about raising her daughter properly and she worried about her health. Lizzie rejoiced when Rev. R.J. Russell arrived in Helena to start a Presbyterian Church, but lamented when her home duties prevented regular attendance. Finally, in the spring of 1872, Lizzie convinced Robert that she needed permanent live-in help. Pregnant again, she could not keep up with the cleaning, sewing, cooking, and entertaining required of her. With the arrival of a second child, her household duties became even more taxing.

Helena, Oct. 14th / 69

My dear Mother:

How natural it seems to seat myself in the old familiar place, writing desk on my knee, and commence a letter thus. Only baby by my side convinces me that nearly a year has elapsed since I sat here and penned for eastern friends the words which assured them of my well-being and happiness. . .

I wish you could have seen us [on our trip west from Omaha], comfortably established in "our sanctum" of Pullman's Palace Car, baby's head comfortably pillowed for a nap on one seat, Rob and I occupying the other, while on various well-arranged hooks hang overcoat, shawls, bonnets and hats; our lunch basket containing a pair of chickens, a duck, sandwiches, apple pies, cake, cheese, pickles, &c., &c. occupying a part of our floor room while in close proximity is our basket of last winter, arranged for baby's linen and now and then a peace flag from the rear of the car. . . .

Saturday we reached Corinne [Utah], the terminus of railroad travel. We find the coach just on the point of starting and, sooner than remain in comfortless quarters here for two days, book our names for departure. . .

And thus we rode on, up hill and down, through wide valleys and across deep streams, stopping often to change horses and three times each day for meals. . . .The second night was a little more wearisome than the first and I was so thoroughly worn out that I slept in spite of all exertions to keep awake. I wish I could picture a coach load of sleeping passengers. It was the most amusing spectacle! Heads bobbing, hats falling off, snores and groans. . . .

Our last night out was the most wearisome since the road was very very rough. Baby and I were about half the time jumping about between coach seat and roof, and I almost thought when we reached the Virginia City junction at 4 A.M. that I could ride no further. But I whispered "home tonight" and watched the fast coming daylight with emotions of pleasure.

At six in the evening we reached Helena, having been driven at the greatest possible rate of speed for seventy-two hours. . . . We bore the journey bravely but are so glad to be home. . . .

Your Daughter,
L.C. Fisk

Helena, Nov. 1st, 1869

My dear Fannie:

[L]et me give you my impressions of life in the metropolis this autumn, of the state of society at the present time and the changes during my absence. In outward appearance Helena has wonderfully improved. The new stone and brick fireproofs erected since last April throughout all the burnt district are much more imposing structures than the hastily erected shanties which the great fire laid low. Among the business firms I notice some new names as well as many old friends, while some. . . have disappeared from mercantile life, the loss occasioned by the fire proving greater than they could bear.

Yes, Helena has "wonderfully improved." I realized it when first I caught a view of the city ablaze with light on the evening of our return, and each day suggest some new comfort and pleasure from its altered appearance. Yet it seems to be all show. I have an undefined impression, for which I cannot give the slightest reason, that all is insecure; that we are resting on the brink of a precipice and the least inadvertence may topple us over. . . . It seems that some terrible calamity is impending. Will the terrible fire again visit us and complete the ruin caused by a whole season of drought and inactivity in mining operations, or will the bubble of outside show and glitter burst, and reveal the emptiness and bankruptcy within? . . .

[Jan. 2nd, 1870]

Yesterday I received calls . . . [and] Baby Grace was a perfect lady on the occasion. . . . You are anxious to know if I treated my callers to wine. No indeed. Coffee flowed freely yesterday, but wine did not. One gentleman told me he had drank twenty cups and had not half completed his round of visits. Poor fellow! If they aren't all bilious for the next six months 'twill not be for the want of strong coffee. . . . Rob paid a number of calls, came home and took an emetic to relieve his stomach.

Nearly every lady in the city kept "open house" and the gents were out in full force. . . .

Baby Grace grows pretty every day. She is trying to creep, but to use an <u>Irishism</u> "advances backward." How much you would love her could you only see her, not only for her sweet face but for her goodness. . .

[Feb. 13th / 70]

Dan [Fisk] took me out to see Mrs. Pinney perform at the theatre the other night. . . . [T]his estimable lady has gone on the stage again. It was her husband's will that she should do so, and she with her two babes, a girl of three months and a boy of a year and a half, who does not yet walk, had no alternative but to obey. Pinney is a tyrant and has abused her shamefully. He is now much reduced in circumstances and proposes to make her bear the burden of supporting the family. Wouldn't I pour hot lead in his ears! She is meeting good success, draws large houses nightly. May it long be extended to her.

I had a long call from Mrs. Gov. [James M.] Ashley one day last week. She is such a funny woman. . . . I must relate one incident in her home life as she told it to us.

Mrs. [G.F.] Gilbert. . . . had been quite ill and one afternoon Mrs. A. walked down to see her, telling her husband before she left home that the dinner was all on the stove ready to be cooked. He had only to tell the children to kindle a fire at the proper time and the meat would steam itself and he could put in the potatoes when the water boiled. She set out on the table the pastry for the meal, and secure in the belief that all was going on well at home stayed with Mrs. Gilbert until quite late.

The first thing which greeted her nose when she opened the front door was the smell of the burning meat. She started at once for the kitchen thinking she might even yet secure it from destruction, but the Gov.'s voice from the parlor said; "Please come here a moment, my dear." She entered to find him reading Mother Goose to the children when he proceeded to render an account of his stewardship.

The children made the fire at the appointed time and "kept it up" as directed. The Gov. seeing things well under way returned to the parlor and soon fell asleep. The children awakened him by blowing in his ears. . . . He heard a great commotion in the kitchen and going out found both doors wide open, the stove red-hot, the meat burned to a crisp and five great hogs disposed in various attitudes about the room. One had knocked down and broken the dinner pot, they had eaten all the pies and bread for dinner, one had licked the kneading board and another was in the tub of drinking water. . . .

With love for all. Good night.

L.C.F.

My dear Fannie:

[On April 30,] was executed that terrible deed [the lynching of
Wilson and Compton], news of which has already reached you. . . . We
watched the crowd about the court house and jail, rushing and surging
to and fro, and although they were as near us as only three blocks up
the street, yet not a sound could we hear. The silence was terrible, the
hush of so vast a throng, [moving] as with one heart and speaking as
with one voice that the men were guilty, and should be hanged at four
o'clock on the old pine tree.

To add to the gloom, and horror it was a dark, drizzly day with
frequent peals of thunder, a day such as we seldom experience here. For
two hours before the executions took place the hills around and opposite
the tree were thronged with people. Women and children were there
and nearly every man in town.

It was a relief when we knew the worst was over, when the misery of
the poor wretches was at an end. . . . It gives me the horrors even now
and I am all alone this evening. . . .

It ill becomes me to set up my opinions contrary to the whole
sentiment of the community in which I live, for . . . our most prominent
men were on the jury which tried and found guilty these robbers and
would-be murderers, but I find it difficult to reconcile these proceedings
with law and order.

There is one fact which should be known ere one can judge fairly in
the case. The excitement of the new mines has brought to our territory
a rough set of men . . . men whose presence in any community is to be
deplored and who can only be deterred from crime through fear of the
most summary vengeance.

Murder and lawlessness were becoming every day more prevalent, a
general feeling of insecurity in life and property pervaded all classes.
Such a lesson as was administered a little more than a week ago may
have been the warning most needed. . . .

[June 15th, 1870]

Our garden 'tis doing as well as can be expected. The [May 30th]
snow storm injured every thing except the tomato plants. We have been
eating radishes from our own garden for nearly three weeks. Peas and
potatoes are in blossom. . . . Corn and beans are somewhat backward.
. . . The flower seeds, too, did not do as we hoped. Many of them are still
below ground. . . .

[July 17th, 1870]

Since I wrote you last the little darling [Grace] has been quite ill,
indeed I was very anxious about her for several days. Her bowels were

in a dreadful condition and I stewed some blackberry with sugar spices, and a little brandy, kept a flannel band about her wet in brandy. These remedies having no effect whatever, we called in Dr. [William] Jones who prepared some aromatic powders, but her stomach could not bear these and for two days even cold water sickened her and was quickly cast up.

The only thing she would take was milk and that I became convinced did not agree with here. I stopped giving it to her altogether (she would not take it scalded) and she speedily recovered. Two days later looking in her mouth I found the eye teeth just peeping through and the stomach teeth badly swollen. No wonder this, added to the intense heat, should make her ill. . . .

We had a terrible scare a few days ago. The corral and stable just above us took fire and for a few moments the wind blew the flames directly toward us. We got all ready to leave at a moment's warning. The whole town was here and many of our friends came in to tell us not to be alarmed, they would save everything for us. Our trunks were brought from up stairs, every dress taken from the clothes-press, and with the silver and other valuables tied in blankets ready to be carried out.

When, fortunately, the wind changed and we were safe. We have not really recovered from the fright yet. The buildings were a total loss to the two young men who owned them. A fire among these tinder boxes is terrible. Had this been on Main St. the whole town must have been sacrificed.

Love for all the family. . .

L.C. Fisk

[In August, Robert Fisk journeyed to the Territorial Capital at Virginia City to confer with the newly arrived governor — Benjamin Franklin Potts. On his return, Robert visited Bozeman and the Gallatin Valley where Lizzie, Grace, and cousin Mae Fisk joined him. While visiting Fort Ellis, Mae met and fell in love with Maj. Eugene Baker. They became engaged, but did not set a wedding date.]

Helena, Aug. 26th [1870]

My dear Mother:

Saturday [August 20] was rendered memorable by the arrival at Bozeman of the Yellowstone party [Washburn-Doane Expedition]. They were all so delighted to see us, not only our old friends but those with whom we had only a slight acquaintance. Our room was at once made headquarters and the hurry and bustle, the noise and confusion can be better imagined than described. The wits of each member of the party seemed to have been considerably sharpened and jokes, puns, and other pleasant wit and rapartee enlivened the hours.

In the evening we had a grand reception of the entire party and a number of officers from Fort Ellis distant from the city two miles. Music and pleasant chat whiled away the hours. At eleven o'clock the company separated to meet again, oh! When? . . . Had Rob been at liberty and the escort a little larger I would have been glad to join the party, and go where no lady has ever yet been. . . .

We had several pleasant rides during our absence and saw much of the lovely Gallatin Valley. Here if nowhere else in Montana, is an abundance of water, the pretty groves skirting the streams. The grain fields, just ready for the harvest were a pleasing sight to the eye long accustomed to gaze only on brown, dreary, mountains. . . .

Among the other officers from the Fort we made the acquaintance of Col. [Eugene M.] Baker of the "Piegan Massacre" notoriety.[2] He is one of the quietest most gentlemanly of men, generous and sensitive. He feels most keenly the many unjust things said of him and his punishment of Indian depredations. He promised to return to Helena with us if we would wait until Wednesday and I partly promised to do so. Monday morning soon after we started homeward he was at the Hotel with his carriage to take us out fishing and afterward to drive at the fort. Montana boasts some of the most genial, hospitable people I have ever met. . . .

[Oct. 2nd, 1870]

Within two weeks I have become a real estate holder; what do you think of that? Rob purchased and gave me a corner lot, one of the prettiest building sites in town. It is on Rodney St. in the block above us. Governor Ashley is building in the same block on the upper corner. We hope to be able to erect a modest little house some time during the winter. Rob has already several thousand feet of lumber. We would like to put up a brick or stone house but can't quite afford it. . . .

My center table is adorned with numerous trophies [from the Yellowstone Expedition] — petrifications, incrustations, bits of alum, of pure brimstone and clear, beautiful agates. I have three of these which I shall have cut and polished for setting.

The brimstone must be pure since it is condensed vapor. . . . The geysers are perhaps the greatest wonders in this wonderful country being the highest known, one rising two hundred and nineteen (219) feet. The falls of the Yellowstone, three hundred and fifty feet high are more grand than Niagara. . . .

Only one event occurred to mar the pleasure of the party and that the loss of Mr. [Truman C.,] Everts. It now seems quite probable that he must have been killed by road agents. . . .

The morning is almost gone. . .

L.C. Fisk

Helena, Oct. 15th, 1870

My dear Fannie:

If you would gaze on a picture of "connubial felicity" . . . just look in upon Rob and I tonight, seated, he with his book and myself with pen and paper. . . .

Speaking of Rob's book reminds me to ask you what style of reading matter I shall send you [at the Freedman's School in Georgia]. We have so many magazines and papers that I have been somewhat at a loss in this respect. I could send all of *Harpers Monthly, Weekly,* and *Bazaar,* also *Frank Leslie's Weekly.* . . . Then I have *Godey's, The Overland* and *Western Monthly, Old* and *New*, a Unitarian magazine, *Wood's Household Magazine, Hearth and Home,* Beecher's paper *The Christian Union,* and one of his sermons each week, besides papers from all parts of the Union. . . .

[Nov. 27th, 1870]

You asked about Dr. Bullard. He is the same kind of friend as of old. We see him less often than formerly as he has more professional duties to attend to. He told me, a short time since, that his practice during the third month after his return amounted to more than three hundred dollars.

His care of and attention to, little Rosa Sands during her illness won him the good will of all the Jews in town and secured him practice in all the families in the neighborhood of Mr. [Morris Sands] who witnessed his attention there.

The little child had congestion of the brain, a most distressing illness. She was first under the care of Dr. [C.E.] Harlow who treated her for mountain fever, got angry and swore at her because she would not take her medicine.

Dr. B. spent every night for two weeks at her bedside. When, at last she died, Mr. Sands came to him with the tears rolling down his cheeks, thanked him for his kindness "which he could never forget and never repay." . . .

70

[Jan. 6th, 1871]

New Year's Day we passed the time very quietly unlike most of our friends and neighbors. . . . I did not attempt to receive calls on New Year's. Our house is so small and inconvenient and I did not feel as if we could well afford the expense to say nothing of the trouble. . . . Receiving calls is a good deal of a farce, under any circumstances. The people you are most anxious to see are sure not to come, and a troop of those for whom you care nothing come in and eat your cake and drink your coffee and never come near you again for a whole year. Such is life.
. . .

Yesterday I scrubbed my kitchen floor on my hands and knees. I usually get a Chinaman or darkey to do it for me but this time I thought I would save the fifty or seventy-five cents. I felt <u>poor</u>. I had just finished when there came a knock at the front door of which baby apprised me in her noisy way.

I threw off my big apron, pulled down my sleeves and opening the door presented myself to the gaze of Mrs. [William] and Miss Chumasero in their velvet cloaks and hats, handsome furs, spotless kids and elegant dresses. Didn't I feel the contrast and for a minute consign them in my thoughts to <u>some other place</u>.

However, I ushered them in, told them this was one of my busy days in the kitchen of which every housekeeper found some, and then I talked as well as I knew how, to atone for the soiled dress and flushed face. Baby had been helping me and did not look very nice and it is my aim to have her always clean. She had cut her finger on a broken toy and daubed her face, dress, and white apron with blood.

These are the times when I long for a [housekeeper]. . . . I am going to astonish Rob some day with an exhibit of the amount of money I have saved him by knowing how to work and being willing, as well as able. My opinion of New England training is more strongly confirmed.

L.C. Fisk

Helena Jan. 22nd, 1871

My dear Fannie:

We are all alone now, Rob having taken a little trip to California [for vacation, and to] Washington. He is trying to secure the appointment of P.M. [Postmaster] for this place and, his papers being all made out, the question arose if it would not be better for him to carry them in person and press his own suit. . . .

Soon I shall think of him as revelling in green peas, asparagus, and fresh strawberries, which the most beautiful country on which eye ever rested is spread out to his unraptured vision. I only hope he will not be so greatly pleased with the country that he will forget to return. . . .

71

Do you know I am getting to be awfully wicked, a regular "heathen Chinee." It is nearly three months since I attended church and that is not the worst of it — I don't want to go. I sometimes get disgusted with Methodism and Methodists and the only way to affect a cure is to stay away from them all together.

The last time I went . . . a young man who used to sing and dance in a hurdy house and was an especial favorite with Daisy Dean (a low, bad, woman who keeps a saloon) read a sort of sermon, prayed, exhorted and sung. That evening has lasted me till now and promises to hold out some time longer.

[Feb. 7th, 1871]

Baby stands in her little chair at the table and chatters incessantly of "damma," "papa," "Ah Mae" (no relative of "Ah Sin"), apples and doggies. . . . She had kept me awake the greater part of the two last nights by her croupy cough. Last night I was up, kindled a fire and heated water to give her a warm bath. It fairly makes my heart stand still to be awakened by that terrible cough. . . .

Mamie Ashley [former Gov. Ashley's daughter] is a frequent, I might almost say constant visitor. She is an original genius and amuses us not a little with her conversation. It occurred to me yesterday while listening to her rendition of Mother Goose's Melodies that the old lady was getting somewhat behind the times, for Rocky Mountain boys and girls at least. She was reading, from the pictures, Tom, Tom the Piper's Son, Stole a pig, &c., and for "crying" substituted "hollering" and added "I suppose somebody licked him."

I question whether it is natural for children to adopt slang or "dialect" as Bret Harte denominates it. Must my little girl soil her sweet mouth with such words and expressions? I hope and pray not. I sometimes think I will bring her home to grandma and let her grow up in the peace and quiet of New England rather than run the risk of making her a fast western girl and woman. We have so few, I might say no, modest pretty girls among those who have lived here for a number of years. . . .

With love. . .
L.C. Fisk

[After two weeks in California, Robert decided his wife and daughter should join him on the eastward leg of his trip. Lizzie and Grace met Robert at Corinne, Utah, where they boarded the Union Pacific for the rest of the journey. While Robert lobbied his application for Postmaster (unsuccessfully) in Congress, Lizzie stayed with her

72

parents. Both Robert and Lizzie hoped construction on their new home in Helena would be complete by mid-summer, but workmen did not finish until September. On reaching Helena in late July, Lizzie described the last segment of their return trip.]

My dear Mother:

Baby was sick all the way from Chicago to Corinne. In the former place she was devoured by mosquitos and the poison from their bites added to change of climate, threw her into a high fever. She depended entirely upon mama, would hardly look at any one else and as a natural consequences, when I reached Corinne I was nearly worn out. . . .

The fearful coach ride from Corinne no pen can describe. The heat and dust, the long, long days and weary night, the want of comfortable food and numerous accidents and delays, all conspired to make our journey almost unbearable. In looking back upon it, one can but wonder that after so many discomforts, life and health are still spared.

To commence, the coach was full and we were compelled to remain a day in Corinne. The evening of our arrival we went directly to the "Metropolitan" [Hotel] and soon retired, but not to sleep. The whole house was so alive with bed bugs that one hardly dared lie down for fear of being carried off bodily.

We were <u>skirmishing</u> all night. . . . Mae and Julia came around occasionally to ascertain if we were still living and we paid them a like compliment. At about two o'clock I went down to the girls' room, found them up and dressed. Julia in bed trying to read . . . had fallen asleep over the book and the bugs were running races over her skirts. . . .

The next day we found [other] rooms . . . and had one comfortable night's rest ere we started on our long ride. We met with many accidents and delays, the horses were poor and fed only on grass and it seemed almost wicked to force them to press on through sand and heat till they were ready to drop. . . .

One little picture of an afternoon ride and I leave my journey. In the valley before us, "Beaverhead," we saw a fearful storm arising and soon the wind and dust swept toward us. The driver handed me the lines while he put on his coat and allowed me to retain them while he used the whip. Our team of four horses was one of the best on the road, and we flew along through wind and dust with ribbons fluttering and shawls breaking loose from pins, even with difficulty retaining our seats on the coach. My bonnet flew off and rested on the back of my neck, my veil went up a thousand feet, and tears ran down my cheeks but amid it all I held fast the lines with the horses galloping furiously. All my fatigue seemed to blow away and the deep draughts of mountain air invigorated me for the rest of the journey.

I never before appreciated the beauties of the main range of the Rocky Mountains which we cross in passing from Idaho to Montana. Everything was covered with verdure, they are up among the rains and snows, many of the peaks are heavily timbered and the roll and sweep of mountain and valley are beautiful to behold. But our journey had an end, and Friday evening at eleven o'clock we drove into Helena.

> Your daughter,
> L.C. Fisk

Helena, Aug. 9th [1871]

My dear Mother:

For the first time in the history of our territory we have a Republican delegate in Congress [William H. Clagett].[3] The news seems almost too good to be true; it is a great, a glorious victory.

The excitement for a week past has been intense. On Thursday last we had a grand demonstration in honor of Clagett; more than sixty wagons and carriages crowded by men, women and children where at [Wasweiler] Hot Springs[4] to meet the honorable gentleman and welcome him to Helena.

We were at the office to see the party enter town and a grand sight it was; bands playing, flags flying, and in the midst rode on quiet little gentleman, apparently the most unconcerned in the group. Baby, who wore "red, white and blue" kissed her hand to him very prettily as he passed and received a kiss in return.

On Saturday evening we were again out in force to hear addresses from Clagett and other prominent Republicans. The balcony of the office (*Herald*) was crowded with ladies as the speakers stand was directly opposite. A band of music on one corner discoursed excellent music. . . . From the roofs of the opposite buildings rockets and roman candles were constantly flying, while a bonfire on either side and Chinese lanterns all about shed light on the scene.

In the street below a dense crowd, swaying to and fro, wild with enthusiasm, keen, and quick to appreciate every argument or flight of eloquence, shouted till they were hoarse for "Billy Clagett." We were home at eleven o'clock, but the crowd did not disperse till three and the boys who remained could scarcely speak next day. . . .

And we have been victorious as we deserved to be. . . . One who has never lived here under rebel rule can hardly estimate the importance of the victory. To see this disloyal element so thoroughly crushed and overpowered is worth all the time and strength expended in the contest.

And to take a selfish view of the matter which was presented me for the first time last evening, the victory is worth about five thousand dollars a year to the *Herald,* in the additional work it brings to them. . .

Your loving daughter,
L.C. Fisk

Sept. 25th [1871]

My dear Mother;

[On] Friday we moved [into our new house.] . . . Suppose you open the gate, come up the walk and enter the front door. The doors are double with ground glass in a pretty pattern in the upper part. You are now in the hall, a cosy little place 7½ x 9½ from one end of which the stairs wind up. We have, so say the builders, the handsomest flight of stairs in the territory.

On the floor is a bright ingrain carpet, under the stairs a little table and hanging on the wall a picture of Niagara [Falls] in all its glory, and a lamp for evening use. To the left you enter the parlor, a bright airy room, wearing ever a cheerful home look; we have a three ply [carpet] for this room, drab, scarlet and green, pure white shades with scarlet cords, and the old furniture.

Here we have a half dozen pictures, all [photographs] but one a fine colored lithograph of two canaries on a spray of wheat. This room is 13½ feet by 16½ feet exclusive of the bay window which is nine feet wide and three feet deep.

From the hall on the parlor we enter the dining room, the same size of the parlor except that the bay window is at the end, instead of the side. Here we have a carpet like that in the hall, green, scarlet and white, green shades at the windows, in the bay window a small round table where stand books and work. A stove, sewing machine, half dozen chairs, with pictures and a clock on a carved bracket complete the furniture.

From the dining room we enter my bed room — 9 x 15 — with one large window. My chamber set fills in very prettily, and here now lies Baby Grace fast asleep. . . .

From the dining we go out on a nice little porch where baby has a swing in which she takes great delight, and from the same room and also from the porch we enter the kitchen the nicest room in the house. It is 16 x 18 feet, has a large pantry and also a bath-room connected with it, a large dish closet near the dining room door, and better than all the rest an unfailing supply of good water.

We have also a good cellar and over the kitchen a nice garret. As we pass up the stairs we come first into a little hall from which we enter the three rooms on the second floor. The largest of these rooms is 11 x

15 and each one of them has a nice closet. We have only one furnished as yet.

We are pretty well settled although there are several little things yet to be done about the house. And now if I could have a visit from my dear father and mother I believe my happiness would be complete. . . .

Yesterday morning at half past four we were awakened by a furious ringing of the door bell, and the fearful news that the *Herald* Office was on fire. So it proved, and we had to stand calmly by and see the labor and accumulations of five toilsome years swept away in an hour....

Not one thing was saved. The fire commenced in the basement which was used as a press room, and smothered and smoked for a long time ere it burst out and was discovered. The building was fireproof with heavy iron doors and shutters; and stone walls on either side between it and the adjoining buildings. Had the fire been kindled any where else all would have been safe. . . .

But we start again, where we commenced four years ago, just as our debts were almost liquidated and we were nearly even with the world.

Nothing was insured except the presses. Those can be replaced and there is type enough in store to start another paper, also a small quantity of ink. The winter's supply of newspaper is between here and Chicago. 'Tis not so bad as it might have been. . . . The loss is probably from fifteen to twenty thousand dollars.

With love to all and many thanks for Fan's letter and picture.

L.C. Fisk

Helena, Oct. 31st [1871]

My dear Father and Mother:

Today, in my mountain home, I am weeping over the sad news [of Fannie's death] only now received; while for two weeks almost, your hearts have been bearing their weight of sorrow. . . . Could I but look upon your faces and try to cheer and comfort you were it only by sorrowing with you. And I shall never see my dear, my only sister again. For her I do not, cannot weep. She has only put off the weary tenement of clay and entered upon the joys of immortal life. . . . She will see her Savior's face, and spend an eternity in joy and praise. But for you, my dear parents, my heart aches, my tears fall. . . .

How thankful I am for the few days we spent together, an unbroken family, last summer. And how glad, too, that Fannie was with you, and her last days of her life were not passed among strangers. . . .

The Fisk house at 319 Rodney Street, 1873. Bundy and Train, photographer. —Montana Historical Society

To God I turn, to His care I commend you, praying that He will bind up your sorrowing, breaking hearts; give you "the oil of joy for mourning."

Your loving daughter,
Lizzie C. Fisk

Tuesday Eve, Jan. 2nd, '72

My dear Mother:

On Tuesday evening the Catholic Fair opened and continued till Sunday morning <u>early</u>. . . . On Saturday evening we went down . . . to be present at the closing of the polls.[5] The contest was very exciting for the last ten minutes. . . . Rob's friends had determined that he should receive the dressing gown made for the most popular editor, and during the last five minutes he received over fifteen hundred votes, and won the dressing gown by seventy-two votes. . . . The contest was, of course, a political one, though at the last it resolved itself into this — Has the banking house of S.H. Bohm, & Co., or the Emma Mine, represented by Charles Dahler, the greatest amount of money at its disposal.

We took the gown, after the vote was counted and declared and came home, and about half past two were awakened by the repeated ringing of the door-bell. The whole party of friends who had exerted themselves for Rob demanded admittance, to congratulate Rob, and see him in his new garment. They gave him three cheers, sang "Home Sweet Home," told stories and finally left, and we went to rest again. . . .

[Jan. 19th '72]

Next week comes the fair given by the ladies of the M[ethodist] E[piscopal] Church. I have taken very little interest in any arrangements for this Fair . . . since I found there was to be dancing connected with the other programme.

We had a Committee meeting some three weeks ago in which the question of dancing was brought up for discussion. Instead of coming out boldly and saying, "We will not have dancing because it is contrary to the discipline of our church, " or else taking the responsibility of the dancing notwithstanding the discipline, it was proposed to let three or four gentlemen run the dance hall and turn over the proceeds to the church trustees. I told the ladies that to me [it was] a very mean way of doing business and at length my patience gave out and I advised them to rent a dance hall on Main Street, employ the hurdy girls and open a faro bank.

The one argument in favor of dancing is, "It brings in more money than any thing else." "Our church is in debt, we must raise money or lose the building." . . .

I must tell you something of the Fair, which commenced a week ago this evening. . . . Much to my surprise, I learned on Tuesday morning, that my name had been placed on the list of ladies to be voted for. I felt a little badly about it at first but as it was impossible to withdraw it I tried to reconcile myself to the notoriety; and I was a little comforted by the assurance from many of my friends that they would not allow me to be beaten. And they were true to their word, and, when the polls closed on Saturday evening, I was three hundred votes ahead of all competition. . . .

And I have been voted the most popular lady in Helena. . . . The stand I took against dancing I think won me some friends and I would not sell or take "a chance" in any raffle at the Fair. People stand by them even though they may not share the sentiments expressed.

In a place like Helena there are of course, many grades of social standing, and I can truly say, without any feeling of vanity, that we stand at the very head. We have not received to our home any gentleman whose moral character was not above reproach simply because of wealth. . . . My time has always been fully occupied and my home duties have been first in my estimation. . . . And so long as our home exerts such an influence I feel that I am doing some good, that my life here is not thrown away. . . .

And now with best love to you and father, I bid you good night.

L.C. Fisk

Helena, Aug. 6th [1872]

My dear Mother:

We have heard and thought of nothing but <u>politics</u> for the last three weeks.[6] Both parties had a band which was drawn from one part of the city to another by six horses, decorated with flags and banners. Early in the day the Union band serenaded us, and some of the neighbors, and about noon they sent up a request for a wreath to decorate their flag staff. We were obliged to take the tops from all our carrots and gather nearly all the flowers our garden boasted, but we made a beautiful wreath and soon we heard them coming. Just as they stopped in front of the gate, up came the rebel band to our next neighbor's and commenced playing "Dixie" and shouting for Maginnis. When the wreath was fastened in its place and the shaft raised, our band discoursed "The Red, White and Blue" and outshouted the other, and then we had rest for the remainder of the day. But I fear Maginnis is elected, although the returns are as yet incomplete. . . .

Col. [Eugue M.] Baker is out hunting Indians with the North[ern] Pacific R.R. Surveying party. There is no possibility that he and Mae will ever be married. When he was here at Christmas, he told her he would be up the last of Jan. or first of February, . . . but he was more than half drunk all the time he was here, and after his return she never heard from him except indirectly, until Rob was down [to Fort Ellis] in February or March, when the Col. told him he hoped to be married some time but was in debt and saw no way of getting out. And we could not but regard that as equivalent to a dismissal of all hope, since he was drinking and gambling worse than ever. Mae waited about six weeks, and, hearing nothing from him and receiving no reply to the letters she sent, she returned his ring bidding him farewell. . . .

[Aug. 25, 1872]

Helena has been visited by another terrible fire and some sixty or seventy buildings laid in ruins, and many families rendered homeless. No person who has not passed through a similar scene can have any idea of the horror it is to see one building after another falling before the progress of the fire while men and women are frantically at work to remove their treasures to some place of safety or to arrest the destructive flames, and yet all seem so powerless.

The wind was raging fearfully all through the fire on Friday and . . . constantly shifted from one quarter to another so that buildings one moment deemed safe were almost the next instant swallowed up.

We were greatly alarmed at first, as we thought the *Herald* Office was again on fire, and [it was] in great danger, [located on] the corner of the block destroyed first, and the fire was on two sides. . . .

[Oct. 20th, 1872]

The *Herald* has kept you informed of all matters of interest transpiring here, has told you all about the [Territorial] "Fair" and the premiums we did not receive as well as those which fell to our lot. Indeed we ought not to complain for we are the richer by a cake basket, a spoon holder and a solid silver napkin ring, while we had nearly enough money in premiums to pay the entry fee.

You will perhaps remember that I assisted in revising the premium list early last Spring; and also in selecting the silver to be ordered from the East. The Fair Association, instead of ordering direct from the manufacturers, commissioned a jeweler here to make the purchases, and as a natural consequence, they were abominably cheated. The other ladies were not much interested and did not find any fault but I had the original list, in the jeweler's own handwriting to show, and the jeweler did not dare refuse to exchange the articles I had drawn for better ones. It was really a very small matter, but it did me so much good to let the old gentleman know I understood his little game. . . . .

Rob's trip [to California, trying to secure a railroad for Montana] was a most delightful one; he is never tired of telling of its pleasures, and though the "traveling gentleman" did not bring a railroad out with them on their return they have since been able to inaugurate measures which we hope will connect us with the outer world in two years time. . . . The offers made by California capitalists were very liberal. For a subsidy of two million dollars they would build a road for us from some point on the Central Pacific, but Montana people think they can build their own road more advantageously.

The "traveling gentlemen" were offered the nice little sum of two hundred thousand dollars, to be divided into four equal parts, if they would arrange matters here to procure the subsidy. They did not accept. We had a rousing railroad meeting here last week, and a committee of one hundred was appointed to confer with the Governor and Mr. Clagett and induce the former to call an extra session of the Legislature to make appropriations toward building a road; and to influence the latter to procure a charter. . . .

With love, believe me, Your daughter,

L.C. Fisk

---

[1]Clark Spence's *Territorial Government and Politics in Montana, 1864-1889*, Urbana: University of Illinois Press, 1975, contains an excellent account of Robert Fisk's relationship with Potts, Sanders and other territorial politicians.

[2]Major (brevet Colonel) Baker led a military expedition against Piegan Indian bands along the Marias River between January 19 and 29, 1870. The campaign sought to punish hostile bands for depredations against white settlers, but it generated controversy over its methods and objectives.

[3]Clagett, a Deer Lodge lawyer, served only one term as Montana Territory's non-voting delegate to Congress. During the Territorial period Montana sent only two Republicans to Congress. Clagett, 1871-72; and Thomas H. Carter, 1888-89. Clagett narrowly defeated Democrat E.W. Toole by 413 votes.

[4]F.J. Wasweiler operated a hotel and bathhouse west of Helena. The spot became more famous twenty years later as the Broadwater Hotel and Hot Springs.

[5]Votes for "The Most Popular Editor" (or banker, or lady) contests cost one dollar each. It was a popular way for groups to raise money. In the case of the editor "election," Republicans like S.H. Bohm supported Robert Fisk of the *Herald*; Democrats supported either E.S. Wilkinson or Martin Maginnis, co-editors of the Democratic *Gazette*.

[6]Democrat Martin Maginnis defeated William Clagett for Congressional delegate -- 4,515 to 4,196.

81

Rufus Clarke Fisk, about 1878. M.A. Echert, photographer.
—Montana Historical Society

The Boys —
Robbie, Clarke, and Asa
1872-1882

*Robbie thinks we have too many boys. He told a
lady not long ago since that his mama "was almost
like the old woman who lived in the shoe."*

(Jan. 29, 1878)

Lizzie's family grew by three during the 1870's: Robert
Loveland (Robbie), born November 28, 1872; Rufus
Clarke, born May 15, 1875; and Asa Francis, born November 11, 1877. Dissention developed between Lizzie and
Robert over naming the second boy. Lizzie preferred
Rufus — a traditional name in her family. Robert insisted
on Lincoln. Lizzie prevailed, but in an apparant compromise, the boy was known as Clarke throughout his life.

Controversies and problems for Montana and the
Helena Herald remained relatively constant during the
decade of the 1870s. Fire continued to ravage the city
along Last Chance Gulch, and a January 9, 1874 conflagration proved more devastating than any of its pedecessors. Over $1 million in damage resulted from a blaze
which originated in the Chinese section of the city — at
the precise spot where the 1869 fire began. Indignant,
many Helena residents spoke out against the Chinese, advocating a block-wide, no-mans-land between Chinese and
Anglo buildings. Cooler heads prevailed and the issue
ultimately dropped from public concern.

National, territorial and local elections continued to occupy much of Robert's attention, and therefore much of Lizzie's. He made a trip back to Washington, D.C. in 1877 to seek Governor B.F. Potts' removal — unsuccessfully — but an 1881 trip produced a Presidential appointment for Robert as Helena's Postmaster — a position he held until 1883.

Every two years the matter of Territorial Delegate to Congress arose. Fisk and the *Herald* championed the forlorn hope of Montana Republicans, only to have the electorate return Martin Maginnis for six consecutive terms from 1872 to 1882. Yet another political issue attracted great attention in Helena during the decade — location of the Territorial Capital.

In 1869, Helena attempted, without success, to secure the capital designation from Virginia City. On August 3, 1874, Montanans again voted on the question, approving the change by 912 votes. When it came to an official canvass, someone reversed vote totals from Meagher County, giving the election to Virginia City and raising accusations of fraud. The investigation focused on Territorial Secretary James E. Callaway, and ultimately the Montana Supreme Court had to settle the matter. In February of 1875, Helena became the capital.

Within Helena, many residents — Lizzie and Robert among them — felt the community should be incorporated or chartered. Repeated efforts proved unsuccessful until 1881. Members of the 1881 Legislature passed a charter for the city, subject to the electorate's approval. Much to the chagrin of opponents and legislators, the charter passed on March 7 and attorneys then discovered that through a wording oversight, the right to vote had been given to all adult citizens — not just adult males as was traditional. Many women anxiously exercised their franchise. Lizzie did not.

Transportation — or the lack of it — continued to bother Montanans. Personally, it meant Lizzie's parents could not come visit her with ease. For everyone it produced long trips by stage or wagon and high freight rates. Railroad supporters divided into three antagonistic camps: one supported the completion of the Northern Pacific; a second advocated the Utah and Northern; a third held out for a local line connecting Fort Benton with Helena and Virginia City. Each group proposed various methods of encouraging railroad building including freedom from taxes, land grants, and territorial or county bonds to subsidize construction. In the end, competition for political and public support was so divided no one triumphed. Two companies did construct — in their own time. On March 9, 1880, the narrow gauge Utah and Northern entered Montana from the south at Monida Pass. By the end of 1881, it arrived in Butte. In December of 1880, the Northern Pacific crossed into Montana from the east. By September of 1883, this transcontinental line was complete.

As white settlers continued to fill the West, confrontations between them and various Indian tribes became more pronounced. Indian raids and warfare attracted much attention among Montana's residents, and Lizzie reflected their views. Lizzie was vacationing back East during the summer of 1876 when the Battle of Little Big Horn shocked a nation busy celebrating the centennial of its independence. No letters recording her reaction to this incident exist. The following year, however, another Indian "war" enveloped Montana and Lizzie wrote home to express her views — typical for the locale.

From June through early October, 1877, Nez Perce Indians, refusing to occupy an assigned reservation in northern Idaho, tried to move to Canada in anticipation of better governmental treatment. The bulk of the flight traversed Montana. Several U.S. Army units pursued them, led primarily by those of General O.O. Howard. On August 9th, troops under General John Gibbon surprised the Nez Perce in the Big Hole region of southwestern Montana. Gibbon failed to stop the Indians and both sides sustained heavy casualties.

A week later the Nez Perce moved through Yellowstone National Park, eluding capture. In the Park, they encountered several tourist groups. Early reports of casualties among the tourists proved greatly exaggerated although the Indians did kill several men. Lizzie described the adventures of the George Cowan party — Helena and Missouri Valley residents. Finally, in late September and early October, U.S. Army units stopped the Nez Perce in the Bear's Paw Mountains, just a few miles short of their Canadian goal. The "Nez Perce War" of 1877 stimulated much discussion and concern in Montana. Lizzie's letters reflect its impact on her relatives and children, as well as her belief that strong action was necessary to quiet the Indians for all times.

The Fisk family had its own triumphs and tragedies during the decade of 1870s. A.J. (Jackie) Fisk married sixteen-year-old Clara A. Wilcox in July of 1873. Van married Alice Reed in February of 1876. A.J. and Clara had two sons — Earl, born in July of 1874 and Ray W., born in October of 1875. Tragically, neither boy lived for more than eighteen months.

Mae Fisk married Charles D. Hard on October 28, 1874. Hard served as a collector for the Internal Revenue Department but soon left government service to enter the livestock business. He purchased blooded horses and raised them in the broad valley north of Helena. Mae had a son, Carl, in August of 1875. As Lizzie watched the families around her, she expressed definite opinions about the new Fisk wives and their shortcomings. Lizzie's own family had its problems, too.

Lizzie marveled that her children remained relatively untouched by accident and illness. Grace, however, contracted scarlet fever in late 1874, and, despite continued medical attention, the illness and its effects lingered for more than a year. Compared to periodic diptheria epidemics and the problems of A.J. and Clara, her concerns seemed small.

Robert Fisk continued to look for profitable investments outside the newspaper field. During 1875, when mining proved unremunerative, several Fisk brothers, along with Dr. C. S. Ingersoll, decided to invest in sheep raising. Van Fisk went to Corinne, Utah, and purchased 1500 head of sheep, driving them back to Helena. East and south of Helena they established Clover Ranch as their headquarters. After some initial optimism and mild success, the venture proved unprofitable, primarily because no one knew how to care for sheep. Much to Lizzie's relief, Ingersoll decided to assume all responsibility for the venture in 1878.

Robert continued to operate the *Helena Herald*, of course. The long hours and meticulous proofreading strained his eyes. His business trips and two outright vacations provided some relief. When Robert left, Lizzie housecleaned — he could not tolerate disorder; she could not stand dirt. Lizzie struggled through a variety of live-in domestics for several years and then, during the summer of 1874, succeeded in getting an eleven-year-old German girl named Mary Knipper. The precise relationship between Mary and the Fisk family is unclear, but they apparently assumed full responsibility for her welfare and upbringing. In return, she assisted with cooking and domestic chores.

Lizzie took some vacation with her family. Between March and July of 1876, she, Robert and the three children traveled east. During their stay Robert conducted business in New York City, and everyone visited the Centennial Exposition in Philadelphia. A.J. Fisk and Clara stayed in Lizzie's home during her absence.

In the fall of 1878, the entire family enjoyed a vacation in central Montana. Finally, in 1880, Lizzie decided she needed her own vacation. She left Robert and Mary with the children and took a week's respite near White Sulphur Springs.

Amid elections, vacations and other excitements, there remained, for Lizzie, the routine duties of a housewife. Mary Knipper assisted, but Lizzie had more than enough cooking, cleaning and sewing to occupy her time. A family of four children (and Mary) was a full time job.

My dear Mother:

During the past week I have been getting well and strong every day, in fact, I feel better now than I have for a year. Grace is quite well again, and Master baby [Robbie] is growing finely. He is just as good as a baby can be, eats and sleeps well, and grows pretty every day. He is such a great, noble-looking boy. I already begin to wish he were not quite so large [twelve pounds at birth], for he makes my arms ache even now. I suppose as I grow stronger I shall feel his weight less. He promises to keep me constantly eating and drinking. . . .

I ought to tell you about our baby's ward-robe. . . . He has Grace's little slips and dresses for common wear and three elegant robes "for high times and Sunday." . . . We have crocheted him an Afghan, at odd moments of time, which I use in his crib. The center stripe is white, and has three embroidered figures upon it, each representing a spray of coral about which a white rose with green leaves has entwined. On each side of the white are salmon stripes, and the outer edge is drab with a vine of blue leaves embroidered in it.

The [cradle] is some of my work. It is a large box, hung on a frame. . . covered with white Java canvas. In the center of the box cover I embroidered a Fuschia pattern and made a band of shaded red leaves about this, and through the middle of the sides and ends. The straps which support the box have the same vine upon them and are held in place by red bows. The inside trimmings are white quilted with red. . . .

[Apr. 20th, 1873]

Have been out this morning on an errand of mercy. Do you remember ever reading in the *Herald* of a little child who ate concentrated lye some three years since? There was . . . an allusion to the fact of his having lived five or six days without nourishment of any kind. Well, the little fellow is dead, his sufferings are ended, thank God, and today he is spending his first Sabbath in heaven.

His throat was so burned by the lye that great ulcers formed and when these healed, left the passage so small that if he took the slightest cold it would close entirely. His poor Mother showed me fifteen or twenty tubes of different sizes which had been used to force open the passage. On one of them, the last used, were the prints of his little teeth where he had bitten it in agony. . . . He was an only child. His parents have been in very good circumstances but have lost everything through the treachery of others. We gave them money enough from the "poor fund" to bury their boy decently and I wish you could have witnessed their gratitude. The mother is a coarse, ignorant, brutal woman and it seemed as if her love for this child was the only human trait she possessed. . . .

Do you still remember the little girl who was burned more than a year ago? On one limb she has still a running sore, and is as yet unable to walk without crutches. When I look upon my two beautiful, healthy, well-formed children how my heart swell[s] with thankfulness. If I can only keep them well. . . .

With best love,
L.C. Fisk

Helena, May 20th, 1873

My dear Mother:

I believe I mentioned in my last letter my intention of cleaning house. On Wednesday morning the white-washers came and commenced work and we also set to work on the carpet. Mary [the housekeeper] had been complaining of a cold on Monday and Tuesday and I had done nearly all the work that she might rest and get well soon. On Wednesday she managed to get the dinner, but Thursday morning. . . . when Mary came down she said she believed she must go to the hospital and rest. . . .

She remarked to a friend whom she met on the way that she thought she would go away till we were through housecleaning; then she guessed I would take her back and she was going to have fifty dollars a month, too. We had previously heard that the servant girls of town intended to strike for fifty dollars a month; and after considering the matter for two or three days, I said Mary shall not come back, and as the servants have organized and prepared "to strike" why may not the mistresses also effect an organization and reduce their servants' wages.

A few anonymous letters sent to myself and a friend raised my indignation pretty high, and I went to work and got all the ladies together and we discussed the question and unanimously decided that after the 1st of June we would pay only thirty dollars a month for help. The ladies are not to be trusted however, and I fancy I shall be the only one who sacrificed anything to the principle. . . .We are still without help . . . and I have written to Deer Lodge for a colored woman but do not know if I will secure her services. The Irish girls are all "down on me," to use a mountain phrase, and I don't suppose I could find one to work for me even for a hundred dollars. . . .

I have to communicate the news of Jack's [A.J. Fisk] marriage which occurred last evening about eight o'clock. . . . It was the funniest wedding I ever attended.

Both parties were elegantly dressed but it seemed like "Sweetness wasted on desert air" to wear such clothes in [Jack's] miserable little log cabin. The bride, as you know, is a mere child in years, not yet seventeen, but she looks and appears like a young lady of twenty-five. She is not pretty but has rather a sweet face, and is extremely conscious of any attractions she may possess. Jack is perfectly infatuated, but Clara — well, she <u>may be</u> in love, but it seems to me she is actuated by purely mercenary motives.

She takes everything as a matter of course, and does not express one word of surprise or delight at anything. Even when she walked into her beautiful new house, which [Jack bought for them to live in after the wedding], . . . she only looked around very coolly and walked into the bedroom, took off her hat and shawl and hung them in the clothes press and laid her gloves in the bureau drawer as calmly as if she had always lived there and had possession of every thing. . . .

She <u>very coolly</u> undressed, and when she was ready for bed called Jack as if they had been married a year or two. Well, as the old lady said, "it takes all sorts of people to make a world, and I am glad I ain't one of them." . . .

[Oct. 22nd, 1873]

Grace is trying hard to be a good girl. . . . [She] is a peculiar child and requires such careful training. She is very bright and active and learns astonishingly fast and, of course, acquires any little disagreeable ways of her playmates as readily as the pleasant ones. . . . She reads and spells quite nicely in words of two syllables, brings in wood, helps set the table and helps in many other ways. . . .

Robbie, the darling, what can I say of him. Fancy a little roly-poly, blue-eyed boy who looks very much like his papa, creeping about the floor like a little sunbeam. . . . A noble head thickly covered with golden brown hair, a high full forehead, . . . a pug nose or perhaps 'tis a stub, a sweet mouth, . . . a dumpling of a figure which persists in outgrowing all the clothes made for it, a pair of dimpled hands, ever ready for mischief, and some sturdy little legs which creep and scramble fast to find it — here you have "our little precious." . . .

Your daughter,
L.C. Fisk

[Helena's last, and most destructive, major fire occurred while Robert Fisk was east on a business trip. Lizzie informed him of the events.]

Helena, Jan. 11th, 1874

My dear Rob:

The telegraph has long since apprised you that Helena is again laid in ruins. The most destructive fire we have ever experienced visited our city on Friday last. . . .

The fire alarm wakened us at about six o'clock on that morning. The wind had been blowing fearfully all night, and many times I had wakened and listened and thought what a terrible time for a fire! And where at last the bells began ringing the sounds became interwoven with my dreams and I did not at once realize that what I dreaded had come to pass.

But I found it necessary to dress hastily and run out to watch the cinders which were falling all about us. We filled all the tubs in the house, and soon Van [Fisk] came up and we begged him to remain with us as Dan had already gone, as 'twould be difficult for us to get out on the roofs. We wanted so much to know where the fire was, that I started out to ascertain and found that only China town was thus far destroyed. . . . From this point they spread with fearful rapidity and people in the International [hotel] barely escaped with their lives.

Then I came back to report and, after quieting the children and taking in Mrs. John E. Blaine's family, went down to the office; found the place deserted, Jack keeping guard over his own house, and then I went up to the corner. There was an engine and the men working it seemed almost exhausted. They had had no breakfast, and could get nothing to drink, and all at once it flashed across me, how good some coffee would taste. . . . I ran home and got over the wash-boilers. On the way I encountered several ladies and they all consented to make coffee also. Then we cut up all the bread the house contained and a large piece of boiled ham and taking some coffee already made started out. Mrs. [Wilbur Fisk] Sanders came directly behind with another pitcher [of] coffee, and not far behind her was Mrs. [William C.] Child.

How gratefully the poor fellows received it. And we were just in time, too, for before we reached the place again, Gen. Blaine's house was on fire and the men had scattered, but after a time we sent them a boiler of coffee . . . other neighbors did likewise. . . .

And our poor city. Will it ever again be rebuilt? Last evening the citizens held an indignation meeting to consider what was to be done with the Chinese. A bill is to be presented to the Legislature setting apart to them certain portions of the city and they are not to be allowed

Helena Herald *office, 1875.* —Montana Historical Society

to build near the habitations of white people. Any buildings they may erect in forbidden ground [would] be considered nuisances and pulled down.

We are quite well at home, except feeling very tired. At one time we feared our house might burn and packed up all our valuables, but we sustained no loss. The *Herald* was equally fortunate, and for all these things were are truly thankful. . . .

Your loving wife,
L.C. Fisk

Helena, May 21st [1874]

My dear Mother:

When I wrote you last we were preparing for Gracie's birthday party; and a very pleasant little party it was. The little girls, to the number of thirteen assembled about three o'clock and had no end of fun and play till six, when tea was served. We had biscuit and butter, cold roast beef, preserved pears, a mold of Jelly, . . . sponge cake and jumbles, and two large cakes, gold and silver frosted. After supper came more games and rompings till sunset, and then the little ones started for home. . . . Grace had all her toys out for the occasion, her dolls appearing in new dresses, her cradle having new pillows and a new cover, white lace over pink cambric. Several of the girls brought her little gifts, and she had a new white dress, a jumping rope and a ball as birthday gifts. . . .

[Grace] is growing quite tall and slender, and has changed in her looks and appearance very much. If I could only keep her away from the many disagreeable, ugly children who infest this part of the town, she should be a very nice girl. . . . We have no public schools here from March to November and nearly all the children in town are turned into the streets to run wild during all these months and they are a nuisance. We have a nice walk all about our corner and carriage steps at the front gate and these are a favorite place of resort. My aspirations are for a house lot ten acres square, with a fence ten feet high all about it, and never a crack through which a child can peep. Perhaps I am selfish, but days and weeks of teaching are all undone by a half hour's play with bad children. . . .

[Aug.2nd, 1874]

The last week has been a very hard one. I discovered Monday morning that Mary [Knipper's] room was getting to be quite densely populated by bed bugs. We had never had one in the house . . . but you can imagine the labors I have since performed in scalding, plastering with quicksilver, &c. I not only gave that room a thorough cleaning and had all the bedding washed but took down every bedstead in the house and used quicksilver and insect powders upon beds and mattresses. I found not even a trace of one except in this room and am quite sure Mary must have brought them here in her clothes. . . .

All this long letter and not a word of "the boy that was born in the house Jack built." He is quite a nice boy I believe weighing about eight pounds. I have only been down once as Clara was so nervous they could not let me come in the house. I did not wish to disturb her, so have not been again. . . .

With love, much love for all,

L.C. Fisk

Helena, Nov. 22nd [1874]

My dear Mother:

I received a letter from Mae last evening, the first since she left [with Charles Hard on their honeymoon]. She tells me their trip as far as Corinne was very severe. They left here Friday morning and only reached Corinne the following Thursday afternoon, tired, sore, and dirty. . . . She misses Robbie more than any one else, as she always called him her baby and used to rock him and pet him more than I ever did. . . .

Have made very good progress with my sewing, too, considering all the interruptions and delays. On Friday I finished off the last of sixteen pairs of drawers for the children; there were eighty-six button holes on the sixteen pair, to say nothing of all the other stitches. . . .

[W]e lost our charter election, . . . and Helena must "try again" before she becomes an incorporated city. It does seem too bad that men of property should be dictated to and ruled by the "roughs" and "rowdies" of a community. But the wrong will some day be righted and for that day we can only wait.

Secretary [James E.] Callaway has been in Helena for a week past having been summoned to appear before the Grand Jury [regarding the recent Territorial Capital election]. The . . . complete returns now detained here by the order of the Judge were decided to be forgeries. Seals, signatures, even the paper on which the returns were made, are false and unlike that originally used.

The writing on the forged returns is said to resemble that of Geo. Callaway a younger brother of the Secretary who left the territory some weeks since. I do hope the perpetrators may be exposed and punished. Mr. [Timothy E.] Collins, the Clerk of Meagher County, was married and brought his bride with him to Helena when he came over to the investigation. I think the young lady who had the courage to become Mrs. Collins under the circumstances deserves much praise, and must have possessed unbounded confidence in her lover. . . .

With love for yourself and father, Your daughter,

L.C. Fisk

[Problems with Grace's health plagued Lizzie during the first months of 1875. Lizzie's own poor health compounded matters, as did the fact she was pregnant — something her parents did not know until the baby's birth.]

Helena, Jan. 17th, 1875

My dear Mother:

Two weeks ago tomorrow Grace's neck commenced swelling and for a week remained in the same condition. During all that time she had a little fever every night and did not gain at all from day to day. Last Sunday night, . . . she was attacked with a violent fever and since that time has suffered much, [and] . . . yesterday one of her ears commenced discharging and today she is almost entirely deaf. We do not know of any way in which she was exposed to cold, and can only think that the disease was in the system and only waiting to develop itself. . . .

To add to our trouble I was foolish enough to go out to Sunday School last Sabbath and as our room was poorly warmed I took a severe cold, and had to stay in bed the greater part of two days. . . . After taking a sweat and binding up my neck in oil silk (an excellent remedy for sore throat or stiff neck) I came out all right and am now quite well. But when our poor little Grace will be well we do not know. . . .

[March 7th / 75]

You will be glad to know that Grace continues to improve in health and strength. She is slowly gaining flesh and really begins to look like herself with rosy lips and cheeks and bright eyes. That she has entirely recovered seems almost wonderful. Dr. [C.S.] Ingersoll has treated another thirty cases of scarletina and scarlet fever during the winter. . . Not one patient has he lost, though there have been deaths in Helena and throughout the territory. One of our nearest neighbors buried her youngest child about ten days since. The little one was sick only twenty-four hours, but none of the remedies used produced the slightest effect. . . .

[March 22nd, 1875]

For a week past I have been suffering from the most severe cold I ever experienced. There has been a kind of episoo [episootic/influenza] going all about town in which I must needs take my share. For the greater part of two days I was in bed and during several more could only speak in a whisper. I had every kind of drink, hot or cold, ever recommended to break a cold and induced perspiration, but the cold was stubborn and would take its own time and way of working off. . . .

I think I have more cares than many mothers with larger families on their hands for I keep my children under my own eye constantly and seldom allow them to visit other little ones. . . . If we have an early breakfast we can generally get the house in order before eleven, and then the children study for an hour before Robbie takes his cup of bread and milk and goes to bed. Then while he sleeps the lessons are recited, the writing accomplished, lunch eaten; and in the afternoon we have a little patchwork or other sewing and then comes play till dinner time. . . .

I have read a good many books this winter from our S[unday] S[chool] and town libraries and have re-read some old ones. Of [Charles] Dickens works I never tire, and hardly know which I admire most. . . . . We have had some excellent German translations, as [John Eugewie's] *Huldah, The Little Moonland Princes* and [Alice MacGowen's] *The Second Wife*, the two former by the author of *Gold Elsie* and *Countess Gisela*. I believe I will send you *The Second Wife* as we and all our friends have read it and I am sure you will like it. It is intense and powerful. These are the only words which describe it. . . .

My letter is long and I bid you Good night.

L.C. Fisk

Helena, May 31st [1875]

My dear Mother:

Was the news of baby's coming a surprise to you? I wonder. I used to fear, during the winter when Grace was so ill and my cares and anxieties were so very great that you might suspect the state of affairs. Even now, as I look back upon that time, I wonder how I ever lived through those days and nights of watching. Holding Grace on my lap for hours each day as I used to do, made me very lame, but that is all going away now and I shall soon feel like myself once more. . . .

And the baby is a nice, plump little fellow [eleven pounds, twelve ounces], just about as large as Grace was and resembling her very much. He takes long naps, scarcely ever cries when awake, and is a very comfortable kind of a baby to have around. Can you not send us a name for this model baby. . . .

And Auntie Mae [Hard] is in [Ft.] Benton, and we hope to see her before the end of the week. "Uncle John" [Fisk], too, has gone down to Benton for his family who were passengers on the steamer *Benton*. The Fisk family in Montana is getting to be quite numerous. . . .

On arriving [at Ft. Benton, John Fisk] found his only daughter and eldest child, [Emma] very ill [with typhoid fever], and wrote us at once that he would be detained for a time as she was unable to travel, though the physician pronounced her improving. The next coach brought her mother [Mary Hamlin Fisk] and youngest brother [Elmer] and the sad news that "Uncle John" was following with all that remained of his daughter. . . .

We made all necessary arrangements for the funeral and on Sunday about six o'clock the little party came in. . . . We feared . . . to open the box which contained the precious dust but found the ice in which the body was packed was scarcely melted and the body there was not changed. It was a great comfort to the poor mother; for when she left Benton and her daughter's still form lying on the bed in the one room which had accommodated them after their arrival there, she took, as she supposed, a last earthly farewell to her loved one.

Poor Emma had been ill since leaving Sioux City. . . . She had had no medical attendance and very little medicine on the long river journey. . . On reaching Benton, she was past all help, but in the midst of sorrow it is such a comfort to her parents that they were able to bring her here and lay her to rest where they can sometimes visit her grave. How much harder it would have been to leave her on the river's bank in that wild Indian country. . . .

[Our] little baby is the best baby I every saw, . . . [but] his name is still a vexed question. I have wished from the first to call him "Rufus Clarke" but papa does not like Rufus though he does not object to Clarke. The name of Paul I would like but for its associations. The little rascal who burned up the Methodist church parsonage &c., was named Paul and he was the worst "minister's son" I ever knew. . . .

[Aug. 8th, 1875]

Jack's boy [Earl] is now lying at the point of death. I have just come from there and my heart aches, my tears fall, for the poor mother as she sits watching her darling child, waiting for, yet fearing, a change. . . . For a week he had been sick with dysentery and the disease is affecting his brain though it has not wholly settled there. He was a beautiful child, large and fair. . . . He lies most of the time in a stupor only rousing when suffering great pain. . . .

[Thursday, Eve, Aug. 19th]

Ere the Sabbath sun had set dear little Earl passed away to his heavenly home. . . . It was hard, oh, so hard, to lay anything so beautiful in the grave, and when we turned our faces homeward I felt as if I could not leave him in that cheerless grave.

My own little ones, how closely I cling to them, and how unstable seem all earthly treasures now that death has once entered our family circle.

[August 13th] brought duties not in the programme, for before night the little stranger so long expected made his appearance. Mae was very sick all day, but when about three o'clock Dr. [J.S.] Glick sent for another physician and a case of instruments my courage began to fail. But fortunately the baby came just in time, although for a few moments we dared not hope he would live. But God was very good and spared him to us, and he is growing and thriving splendidly. His name is Carl Bowen, he weighs nine and one-half pounds and resembles papa. . . .

Mr. Hard has purchased a ranch about five miles from town and will build there this fall. He goes east about the first of October to bring out more stock. Van is still on the road between here and Corinne. We hear from him occasionally, but with fifteen hundred sheep to look after he is excused from writing many letters. . . .

The hour is late and my eyes are heavy.

L.C. Fisk

[In mid-March, 1876, Lizzie and Robert took the children east. He attended to business and political matters, while everyone enjoyed a visit with Lizzie's parents and a tour of the national Centennial Exposition in Philadelphia. During their absence, A.J. and Clara Fisk lived in Lizzie's home. Also during this period, Clara Fisk gave birth to her second child, Ray. Robert, Lizzie and family returned to Helena late in July.]

Helena, July 30th [1876]

My dear Mother:

It is pleasant to be seated once more in the old place, and to commence a letter in the good old way. . . . I have tried to be charitable and make every allowance for Clara. Her baby [Ray] was very sick all the time she was here, and she had no help but a Chinaman who would not sweep a room or make a bed. That poor baby! It seems as if 'twould be a mercy if were taken away from its suffering. It has some kind of a skin disease. I don't know what to call it but many, who do not hesitate to call things by their right names, pronounce it scrofula. It is and has been one mass of corruption. The only way in which they can keep it comfortable and prevent hard scabs from forming is to cover it with oil silk even to its feet and hands. The itching is so great that his hands are kept bound to his sides to prevent his scratching. Is it not dreadful and they have no hope that he can be well or much better until he gets all his teeth. It is hard for the little one and yet more trying for the parents. . . .

[Sept. 7th, 1876]

Van's house [at Clover Ranch] is greatly improved and is as pleasant and convenient as one need wish. His wife [Alice Reed] is very discontented and makes herself and husband very unhappy, but I do hope she will make up her mind to settle down with her husband and make the best of things as they are. She has foolish notions in regard to being in town, dressing, and attending dancing parties. If she could only be made realize that the weal or woe of all her future life depends on her conduct now! . . . I hope Van has not made a mistake.

I wonder if I had better tell you of my experience in getting ready for our ride [out to Van's house] . . . . I had made every preparation possible the night before, but the morning proved cool and cloudy and we needed more heavier clothing than I had laid out. I wanted my winter cloak . . . and made a visit to the closet where it was hanging, but . . . I was called down stairs . . .

I made a second attempt and just as I reached the closet door I heard a splash, a scream and a fall. Down stairs I rushed and baby, who was dressed nice and clean and ready for a start came dripping from the bedroom. He had pulled the water pitcher from the washstand. . . . The third time I secured the cloak and rushed down stairs to find that Robbie had knocked the pin from the faucet where we turned on the water in the door yard and thus cut off our supply in the house. The pin and handle lay at the bottom of the box and water was two feet deep. . . So I had to go "a-fishing" and shut off the water here, before I could get water enough in the house to wash my hands. But we were finally started and enjoyed our ride and visit greatly. . . .

[Dec. 31, 1876]

And now I come to a sad story. . . . We had just fallen asleep when there came a violent ring at the door and Jack's voice shouted "the baby is choking to death." Rob dressed and ran for the doctor . . . and I went down there as quickly as possible. The poor baby had been sick for a week. . . . [T]hey had changed physicians and medicine, and they learned when it was too late they had been giving him mercury and iodine in a solution of arsenic. . . . His papa raised him to give him his bottle and he choked so badly that they thought he would never breathe again. Still he lived four hours in the most fearful agony, his eyes were rolling, his jaw set, his every muscle tense and twitching, and the secretion of saliva, mucus and whatever streaming from his mouth.

99

Jack and Clara stayed by him and held him till they could bear it no longer then Jack gave him to me and I held him till he died. . . .

Dr. Ingersoll attributed his death to salivation. I have a different theory. Rob won't let me say it here but I may whisper it to you. The poor baby was diseased through and through, with something of a scrofulous nature, and this disease which had almost entirely disappeared on its body had only gone in till it reached throat and lungs. There were hard knots or lumps on every cord of its neck and I cannot conceive of anything human with a worse looking face than the poor baby had when it died. I thank God every hour that its sufferings are over, and I do hope I may never see such suffering again.

Jack and Clara are again left desolate. . . .

With love for all,
L.C. Fisk

[Feb. 8th, 1877]

My dear Mother:

Our new minister [Rev. J.D. Hewitt] is expected to arrive this evening with his wife. I hope they will be people whom we will like, who will be able to accomplish much good here, and I do hope most earnestly of all that they will have a mind and will of their own, and not allow themselves to be toadied, and in the end, spoiled. . . .

Our wise legislators seem as yet to be doing little to help along the project in which we are all most deeply interested — the railroad. There is so much jealousy among the members from different sections of the territory that we fear the whole session is to be spent in idle quarreling and that our hopes for the beginning even of a railroad are to be laid over for two years longer.

I do not feel as if we would remain here a great while longer without rail communication with the outer world, though we would perhaps sacrifice something in leaving. . . . [I]n a few years our children will need better educational advantages than Montana can offer, and I could not think of sending them three thousand miles from me. . . .

[July 5th / 77]

[I]n regard to our new minister, I cannot say that I am charmed with him, though I believe he is acceptable to the majority of his people. Socially he is a decided success, can and does make himself agreeable to everyone, and in this way makes many friends. He has a fund of good, practical common sense and genuine Scotch shrewdness . . . which stand him in good stead in his labors here. Occasionally he preaches a good sermon, but his voice is bad and his manner and gestures more forcible than eloquent or graceful. I ought not to criticize, he is trying hard to do a good work here. Our congregation and Sunday school are very small this summer.

The boys on the ranch are just through sheep shearing. They are all agreeably disappointed in the yield of wool, there being five hundred pounds more than was expected. The ranch is self-supporting this year, and if properly managed ought, hereafter, to bring in a nice income. . . .

With much love from all,
L.C. Fisk

Helena, Aug. 16/77

My dear Mother:

The Indian news from Montana of course reaches you. I sincerely hope you are not disquieted thereby, or suffering anxiety on our account.

I have been so glad that Gen. [John] Gibbon struck a decisive blow [in the Big Hole Battle] at these thieving, murderous bands who wanted to pass peaceably and quietly through our territory this year only to return upon us another season and repeat the outrages perpetrated in Idaho a few weeks since. We are safe from those Indians only which have been sent to "the happy hunting grounds." . . .

The children are greatly interested in the Indians and Indian news: Robbie has found in the garret an old sword, which he wears almost constantly, and with which he fancies himself able to meet and fight any number of Indians. His sword loses something in his estimation from the fact that it is not sharp enough to cut anything, but he assures all his friends that the point would "stick in to any Indian and kill him quicker!"

War is so cruel; and it does seem that to be shot down by savages is almost throwing one's life away. Any one of those brave men who was sacrificed in the Big Hole battle was worth more than all the Indians in the country, and yet every year thousands of just such men are slain and our "Indian policy" remains, not unchanged but ever changing for the worse. The only comfort, and only safety, of the extreme West lies in total extermination of the savage. . . .

[Aug. 28th, 1877]

For the last three weeks we have been living in the midst of constant excitement and anxiety. . . . [Y]esterday afternoon dispatches were received from Bozeman stating that parties of tourists had been attacked in Yellowstone National Park and sixteen persons killed by the same hostile Indians. . . . But this evening comes more cheering news. The camp was surrounded and fired into by the Indians, several being wounded and two or three killed. Those who were able to do so

Grace Chester Fisk, 1877. —Montana Historical Society

fled to the brush and were not pursued and have nearly all been heard from. . . .

We had our own individual trouble, too, for all the Fisk families in Missouri Valley came rushing to town Saturday night thinking or pretending to think, that there was danger there. I don't suppose there was an Indian within one hundred and fifty miles of them but they got up "a scare" and ran away from imaginary dangers. On Sunday I had a family of ten to cook for and I had planned a nice quiet day. . . . Such a noise and commotion, a rushing hither and thither, to say nothing of the being routed out in the middle of the night to make beds, made me pretty nearly sick. . . .

[Sept. 11th, 1877]

The Indians just now are quiet or rather they have gone so far away that we cannot hear from them and have reached a section of country where there is no one for them to molest. Nearly all the Yellowstone excursionists have been found, all except two alive and well.

It is difficult to understand why the Indians did not kill them all when they had the power to do so, but the warfare of these Indians has been unparalleled in history. The Nez Perce warriors seem civilized in a measure, and, like the South in the days of the Rebellion, "only ask to be let alone.". . .

School opened a week since. Grace has a new teacher, is promoted one class and doing finely. With Robbie I had a battle to induce him to go, and just as he had begun to like it the decree went forth that no pupils were to be admitted under six years of age. . . . He will learn quite as rapidly at home, and certainly acquire much less evils.

Our best love to Grandpa and Grandma.

L.C. Fisk

Helena, Oct. 28th, 1877

My dear Mother:

Perhaps you would like to know if I am pleased with the prospect of an addition to my cares [pregnancy]. I did <u>not</u> want any more children, and there have been times in the last few months when I have felt <u>utterly unreconciled</u> to the state of affairs, and even now I sometimes think I cannot care for any more little ones; but I try to recall the old proverb that "the back is fitted to the burden," and come to believe that strength will be given for every duty.

My children are so strong and healthy, so perfect mentally and physically (a mother's fond partiality of course) that I can hope they will prove a comfort to me and be of some use in the world. So I have summoned philosophy and Christianity to my aid and come to feel like myself once more, I will not complain. . . .

[Dec. 2nd '77]

Little Asa Francis is a good baby, spending all night and nearly all the day in sleep. He already begins to look about and notice different objects so that when awake he will sit in a chair for a few minutes at a time and require no tending. If he were not so good I do not know what we could do with him or with the rest of the little ones. . . . Though every evening finds me weary, the night's refreshing sleep prepares me for the next day's duties and I can rise with a brave heart to enter upon them. . . . .

[Jan. 29th / '78]

Rufus Clarke came to me a few days since bringing a little roll of Arnica Plaster. I said "Where are you hurt?" thinking there was another sore finger demanding my attention. He said in reply, "No, no, mama, put it over the little baby's mouth so he can't cry and spit milk.". . .

Robbie thinks we have too many boys. He told a lady not long since that his mama "was almost like the old woman who lived in the shoe," and promised the lady that he would come and live with her and be her boy. When I heard his plans I said "Why Robbie, would you go away and leave mama?" He sprang to my side and throwing his arms about my neck gave me one of his "bear hugs" and hastened to assure me over and over again that he was "only fooling." . . .

[March 25th, 1878]

I am never lonely or dull. Our children leave me nothing to long for in the way of noise or excitement. Flute, fife and drum are sounding often before breakfast; or a coach is built; a campaign against the Sioux Indians planned; or a trip to the Yellowstone arranged. And all day long they never tire or falter. . . .

Have you seen or heard (I hardly know which term is correct) the telephone? We were invited one evening a few weeks since to meet a party of friends at Prof. [H.P.] Rolfe's to witness some experiments with this instrument. The machine is very simple. Only a mouth piece and ear trumpet attached to the brass wire which they had been accustomed to use in telegraphing. The wire made a circuit of about three miles connecting the house of another friend and where also a party was assembled. By applying the ear trumpet or cup to the ear, we could hear and distinguish voices in conversation, singing, &c. . . . With a little improvement we (you and I) will yet be enabled to visit with one another across the continent.

The voice or sound transmitted is most peculiar and unearthly. I can think of nothing like it. It seems to come from the depth of the earth. I fancy the still, small voice the prophet heard must have been something like this. . . .

With love for all,
L.C. Fisk

Helena, Sept. 16th, 1878

My dear Mother:

We are all once more safely at home after journeying for ten days through the loveliest part of Montana. . . . The White Sulphur Springs, the point toward which we were aiming, is distant from this part of the Missouri Valley about seventy miles. The route lies first down the Missouri Valley about fifteen miles, through the finest grain growing section in Montana. The farmers were all busily engaged in harvesting their crops. We saw in successful operation every variety of labor saving machinery, reapers, binders, threshing machines, &c. I could scarcely believe it possible that there were people enough in Montana to consume all the grain we saw in this valley, and this of course but a small part of that produced in the territory.

After leaving the valley our way lay by a winding mountain road into Diamond City. The hills we climbed were high and very steep, the slightest accident would have sent us rolling down the most frightening precipices. . . . At Diamond we spent the night and drove the remaining forty miles to the Springs the following day. . . . As we ride along, the peaks tower far above us, their summits covered with perpetual snow, while the smaller and nearer mountains are heavily timbered, and in the morning sunlight every tree glistens with the white frost of the previous night. Soon we reached the summit of the divide; but just as we commence to go down on the other side a broken bridge arrests our progress. . . . We all alight, unload the buggy, unhitch the horses and lead them, one at a time, across the upper part of the bridge which has not yet settled. Then papa and I draw the buggy over, take across the babies and load, harness and start on.

We . . . call for a few moments at Camp Baker[1] for a chat with friends among the officers, and then are again off for the Springs. From Camp Baker to the Springs is a distance of eighteen miles. We make the drive in two hours and twenty minutes.

Here a nice room with two beds is placed at our diposal, a warm fire is made, for the evening is cool and after supper we all try a Sulphur Bath. I can't say that I like to be scalded at any time, and certainly not

105

in water which smells as this did, nor could I drink it as most of the visitors did, two glasses before every meal. It may be if I had been an invalid I should have been able to do so with greater zest.

But I did enjoy the fishing and more fully still, the fish, after they were caught and cooked. What could be more delightful than a fine mountain trout weighing say two pounds, freshly caught, nicely broiled and served quite hot. These with good tea and coffee, excellent bread, oatmeal and other like dishes constituted our "living." Rob shot several grouse and pheasants, and these also were nicely served.

One afternoon as we were riding over the mountains our horses began to lag and to look longingly down at the water which was trickling over the rocks far below. We had no means of giving them a drink until we espied a miner's cabin nestled in a little sheltered nook beside the road. Just opposite, where the water fell over the rocks into a little basin stood a pan of potatoes evidently intended for the supper of "ye honest miner." We poured potatoes and water out upon the rocks and borrowed the pan long enough to give both horses a good drink. It seemed impossible to satisfy them; the water was clear as crystal and ice cold, and when we had tasted we wondered not at their eagerness.

I must not forget to add that we returned the potatoes again to the pan and covered them with water as before, and were moved to leave with them a note of thanks. . . .

My letter is too long to add more than our united love.

L.C. Fisk

Helena, Feb. 17th, 1879

My dear Mother:

Grace's [classroom] is . . . blessed with a most excellent teacher, Mrs. D.M. Darnold. She teaches because she loves the work, though she has a husband both able and willing to care for her. She is a lady ever and always and I feel assured that Grace is not learning from her that which she must unlearn at home. But the children with whom she comes in contact are with few exceptions, ignorant, vulgar, uncouth, "full of all subtlty [sic] and mischief."

Robbie's teacher has one idea ever uppermost, which is that she is getting on in years and is still unmarried. She has "set her cap" for each and every one (in succession) of the eligible bachelors in the place, thus far to no avail. She is a good hearted woman but not at all smart, indeed I don't believe she has an average amount of common sense. . . . One can plainly hear "the sound of the machine" among the flowers in her garden. She thinks teaching "such hard work" and works for the money that she may rival in dress some of her friends. . . .

[Lizzie's estimations of Helena's school teachers changed the following year.]

[Feb. 19, 1880]

I do not intend sending Grace and Robbie to school again this winter. . . . I have long been dissatisfied with the school. Mr. [R.J.] Howie, the Principal, is an excellent Christian man. Grace's teacher, Miss [Helen P.] Clark,[2] is a half-breed Indian, the daughter of Malcolm Clark, who, you perhaps remember, was killed by the Indians nearly eleven years ago. Miss C. was educated in a convent and is avowedly a Catholic, but she has no faith in God or man. She <u>hates</u> the school, <u>hates</u> her work. While I am sorry for her, she is not the person I would choose as an instructor of my children.

Robbie's teacher is a divorced widow, a person of no education that I ever heard of. I think she does work very hard in her school, but she does not "know how" to teach successfully. I would like to see a half dozen Yankee teachers filling positions in our school, young ladies educated thoroughly for their work. . . .

[May 19th /80]

Rob has had so many trees planted this spring. . . . There are Maple, Beech, Birch and Mountain Ash, and an Arbor Lilac. We had already put out a dozen fruit trees, mostly cherry, two dozen currant bushes, six grape vines, a half dozen each English Gooseberry and Blackberry bushes. . . . When you remember that all this plantation has to be irrigated, you will understand the labor attendant upon gardening in Montana.

We have no rain or snow to wet down more than a couple of inches but the supply of water is this year abundant. We have in addition to the hose which connects with the hydrant, an underground ditch flowing past the roots of most of our trees. . . .

[H]owever strongly we may be attached to this western world we cannot deny that we are here deprived not only of many luxuries but even of comforts. So many advantages of society and culture and opportunities for mental improvement are beyond our reach. Ah! well, let me not think of these but rather of the many blessings of my lot.

L.C. Fisk

White Sulphur Springs,
August 15th, 1880

My dear Mother:

Do not be surprised at the date and heading of my letter; I have only run away from home for a little rest and play-spell. The children are all at home taking care of their papa, or sharing his care. . . .

I had been planning a visit to the Springs all summer and felt that I could no longer delay. . . . So on Friday last . . . I set out in the coach. . . . Yesterday I rested all day and today, Sunday, I am of course very quiet. Tomorrow I am going fishing, when I expect to distinguish myself. A gentleman went out about two miles from here yesterday and returned in a few hours with over sixty nice fish. . . .

I do find it very pleasant to be here; free from care and nothing to do but rest and enjoy myself. . . . I do not know how long I can be content here, but I do need the rest and change and shall try to be happy as long as possible. . . .

[Helena, Sept. 16th, 1880]

Since Tuesday noon we have awaited so anxiously news [about the] elections. . . . Col. [W.F.] Sanders once more leads the forlorn hope of the Repulicans in the Territory.[3] I believe he is almost sure to be defeated, but should he be victorious the Republican party of Montana deserve what they will most surely receive for placing such a man in nomination.

Treacherous, crafty, thoroughly unprincipled, he will sell himself and friends at every crisis, and then boast of his achievements. Who would be a politician! . . .

[Mar. 31st, 1881]

Now that our city is incorporated we hope it may be thoroughly cleaned and that people will not be allowed to throw refuse matter of all kinds into the street. According to the provisions of the Charter, ladies are entitled to vote for city officers. This was not intended on the part of those who framed the document, but was only owing to some oversight on their part. Some of my lady friends are quite anxious to avail themselves of the privilege and we talk of making up a party to go "to the polls." I must own for myself I am not at all desirous of claiming this privilege but I may perhaps go to gratify some of my lady friends who have no one to do their voting for them. . . .

I must not write longer tonight. The hour is late.

> With love,
> L.C. Fisk

[1]Camp Baker (1869-1880) was a small military installation on the Smith River. The post moved upstream in 1870 to a location near the mouth of Camas Creek and changed names in 1878, becoming Fort Logan, in honor of Captain William Logan who died at the Battle of the Big Hole, August 9, 1877.

[2]Helen P. Clarke later became Superintendent of Schools for Lewis and Clark County. The death of her father, Malcolm Clarke, precipitated a retaliatory expedition against the Piegans by Major Eugene M. Baker, which, in turn, generated considerable controversy.

[3]Democratic incumbent Martin Maginnis won his fifth term as Delegate to Congress in 1880, defeating Wilbur F. Sanders -- 7,779 to 6,281.

James with dog Trilby, Florence, Stanley, Grace, Bob and Asa, 1895. —Montana Historical Society

Twins and Troubles —
Florence, James and Mr. Bryan
1882 - 1891

I was not ready for one baby and when two came thus
prematurely upon me . . . I felt entirely unreconciled
to the thought of such an addition to my cares.

(May 14, 1882)

Lizzie Fisk gave birth to twins Florence and James on
April 24, 1882. Although not pleased at the prospect of
having more children, Lizzie welcomed them as she had
the others. Again Lizzie and Robert disagreed over names.
Lizzie considered calling the girl Mae Bushnell, after Mae
Hard who named her daughter Bessie in Lizzie's honor.
She settled on Florence Rumley, however. James (or
Jamie) had the middle name Kennett, although in later
letters Lizzie called him James Garfield and James
Rumley.

Now faced with raising six children — and she gave
Robert little credit for assistance — matters of house size
and household help became all important. The Fisks
enlarged their home the year following the twins' birth,
and Lizzie pushed repeatedly for improvements and
finally a new house altogether. Robert consented (grudg-
ingly) to improve their Rodney Street home — adding
electric lights — but steadfastly refused to consider
moving.

Mary Knipper proved invaluable to Lizzie in the years immediately following 1882. But, in Lizzie's words, "she came of age," and on February 24, 1886, wed Clifford Anderson. The couple moved to Butte for a year and then returned to Helena where Mr. Anderson worked for a variety of real estate firms. Replacing Mary was not easy. From the spring of 1886 through May of 1887, Robert's second cousin Mary Fisk stayed in Helena and paid for her room and board by cooking and cleaning. When she left, Lizzie looked for a satisfactory replacement whom she never found. Undoubtedly, she expected much and paid little. At one point, because of the frequent turnover in domestic help, Lizzie resorted to numbering maids to avoid confusion.

Grace, Robbie, Clarke and Asa grew up, too. Long frustrated with what she felt was the crude and boisterous environment of the west, Lizzie convinced Robert to send Grace back to a private school (Carleton) in Northfield, Minnesota, during 1884. She stayed there but a short time when Lizzie became very ill with fever, rheumatism and gout. Grace returned to Helena during the winter of 1884-1885, cared for her mother, then went back to Minnesota and finished out the school year. After completing the 1885-1886 term, Grace decided she had had enough education.

Back in Helena, Grace helped around the house or tried her hand at art and various odd jobs. In 1888 she even thought about buying her own home. In truth, Grace enjoyed Helena's social life — as much as her mother permitted — and became increasingly self-reliant.

Robbie also went away to school — Shattuck Military Academy in Faribault, Minnesota. He stayed and appeared to enjoy two years — 1886 and 1887 — before his father decided private schooling was too expensive. Robert put his son to work at the *Herald* and Robbie began a career in journalism which lasted almost thirty years. After finishing eighth grade, Clarke enrolled in a Helena

111

business school and secured work with various firms, including the Montana Phonograph Company. Clarke and Asa both sold newspapers as well, and later worked part-time for their father. In 1890, Clarke also went away to school — a private military academy in Ogden, Utah, operated by C.L. Howard, the former superintendent of schools in Helena. Clarke liked the academy and did well.

The health of Lizzie's parents began to decline during the 1880s. She succeeded in convincing them to visit Helena from July to September of 1883 and had Robert call on them whenever he went east for business, pleasure and politics. During September and October of 1889 Lizzie decided to go back to Connecticut on her own. She took Grace and left Robert with the care of the other children.

Transportation in and out of Montana improved greatly during the decade. The Northern Pacific reached Helena from the east in late June of 1883. Lizzie's parents used the line for their visit. By the time they left in September, they could travel over the Continental Divide west of Helena and connect with the Montana Union/Utah and Northern through Garrison. Lizzie accompanied them as far as Silver Bow, near Butte, stopping along the way to enjoy the wonders of Gregson Hot Springs.

Railroads fanned out from Helena after 1883, and yet another line entered the city in 1887 when James J. Hill pushed his St. Paul, Minneapolis and Manitoba Railroad into Montana. A branch of that — the Montana Central Railway — reached Helena in November of 1887, and Butte two years later. Helena also acquired street railway transportation. In 1886 a single horse car line connected the business district with the Northern Pacific depot one mile north of town. By 1889 several lines joined all parts of the city, including the newly constructed Broadwater Hotel. Located a few miles west of Helena, the facility included a 100x300 foot indoor pool (or plunge) — reportedly the world's largest at the time.

To her already substantial home duties, Lizzie added other interests. She became involved with the Women's Christian Temperance Union (W.C.T.U.), but withdrew when prohibition threatened to become a political issue and split the Republican Party. She also participated in the local Poor Committee, and visited the "Poor Farm" in the Helena Valley, bringing religion and cheer. Her efforts to improve conditions of women in Helena and Montana spurred her to support what became the predecessor of a Y.W.C.A., and to appear before the Territorial Legislature. She lobbied for reform in rape and seduction laws. Both bills she favored ultimately passed.

As always, Lizzie's letters relfected the interests and activities of her husband and the other members of the Fisk family. In 1886, Van Fisk purchased a small weekly newspaper called the *Townsend Tranchant*. The paper had begun three years earlier in a farming community thirty miles south and east of Helena. Van continued to publish the paper until his poor health forced its closure on January 23, 1890. He came to Helena for medical help, but died on April 19.

Robert became active in the Grand Army of the Republic and the Montana Press Association — serving as the president of the latter organization in 1889. In the interest of both groups, he traveled around the state and to various national conventions. Sometimes he traveled alone, but as the children grew, he frequently took them along. During one of these trips, in 1888, Lizzie was alone at home when the house was burglarized.

Robert and the *Helena Herald* continued to be involved in Montana's major political issues. In 1884, Grover Cleveland won the Presidential election — the first Democrat to hold that office since the Civil War. The change brought a shuffling of political appointments in the territories. Robert lost his postmaster appointment. Montana received its first and only Democratic Governor — Helena banker Samuel T. Hauser. More Democrats filled other

113

positions. Some appointees were southerners, much to the disgust of the Fisks and other Union veterans.

Local political issues did not escape Robert's attention either. When dirt and worms began to flow from Helena's domestic water supply, he accused the Helena Water Company of bad service and monopolistic operation. He championed the cause of George F. Woolston's competing corporation. In time the City Council licensed both firms. Quality and cost improved. A schism in Montana's Republican party produced competing newspapers; first the *Record* then the *Journal*. These hurt *Herald* sales and threatened Fisk's printing patronage. At one point the competitors offered to buy out the *Herald*, but Fisk refused. He managed to survive the challenge but began to weary and looked forward to retirement.

Statehood was the major political issue of the decade. The question came up in 1884, but a partisan Congress turned down the proposal. In 1888 the outcome appeared more auspicious. That year, for only the second time since its formation in 1864, Montana elected a Republican delegate to Congress. Thomas H. Carter defeated the Democrat William A. Clark, 22,486 to 17,360. Clark, one of Montana's millionaire "Copper Kings," spent a considerable amount of money on his unsuccessful campaign.

Republicans won nationally in 1888. As a result, in February of 1889, a lame duck Congress and outgoing Democratic President Grover Cleveland approved an Ominibus Enabling Act which provided for the admission of several western states — Montana included. Montana held a Constitutional Convention from July 4 to August 17, 1889 in Helena; prepared the necessary document; and presented it to the people on October 1st. The outcome of the voting was a foregone conclusion. By November, 1889, Montana had statehood.

Unresolved was the question of a location for the permanent state capital. The Constitution mandated an election in 1892 where any city could be a contender. When no

114

community received a majority of the votes, the two top vote-getters — Helena and Anaconda — had a run-off in 1894. After intensive campaigning Helena secured the permanent designation.

Social as well as political issues arose and Lizzie's letters illustrated her strong convictions. In November of 1884 a notorious criminal named Jack Redmond — better known as Con Murphy — escaped from county jail. On January 26, 1885 a posse under the leadership of Helena Police Officer George Bashaw captured Murphy 14 miles south of town. The prisoner attempted to escape, wounding Bashaw. As the party entered Helena, a mob of several hundred men met them, took the prisoner, and hanged him from a railroad bridge. On his body the mob pinned a note which read "3-7-77 Beware" — symbolic warning to other outlaws, developed out of earlier Montana Vigilante activities in 1863 and 1864. Lizzie tacitly approved of the action.

In March of 1886, millionaire mine owner Thomas Cruse married a woman nearly forty years his junior. Lizzie did not approve. She and Robert received invitations, but at her insistence, they did not attend. Like her strong opposition to liquor, Lizzie remained steadfast in her principles.

Throughout the controversies and politics, the domestic help and the household duties, Lizzie remained foremost a mother. She attempted to raise her children as best she knew how, preparing them for successful futures. In 1890 Lizzie's frustrations peaked.

George Hardy Bryan came to Helena in 1889, working briefly as a surveyor, then as a bookkeeper at the Broadwater Hotel. Not long after his arrival he met Grace Fisk and soon became a frequent visitor at the Fisk home. The attractive, twenty-year-old miss was not without other suitors; among them Walter S. Kelley, an assistant at the U.S. Assay Office. Both Kelley and Bryan proposed to

Grace (and according to Lizzie's letters there was at least a third competitor).

In an attempt to dissuade Grace from marriage, Robert and Lizzie bought her a piano and financed her expensive China painting hobby, but in August, 1890, Grace announced that she and Hardy Bryan were going to be married on September 17th. Lizzie and Robert objected, but their protest delayed the ceremony only two weeks. October 1st Grace and Hardy Bryan married, with only Dan Fisk and Robbie as witnesses at a brief civil ceremony. Neither the Fisks nor the Bryans made the event public, for none of the three Helena dailies carried any notice of the marriage. Robert and Lizzie refused to attend.

For a brief period after the wedding, Hardy and Grace lived at the Broadwater. When the hotel closed for the winter, he secured a bookkeeping job with the Helena Gas, Light and Coke Company. Financial trouble forced them to seek ever cheaper residences. During the first year of their marriage they lived in at least five separate locations, including an old home owned by Charles Hard, the Robbie Fisk home during August of 1891 (much to Lizzie's disgust), and finally a small place on Rodney just a block away.

The first year of marriage also saw the birth of a son on July 1 — Charles Stanley Bryan. Now a grandmother, Lizzie mellowed somewhat toward Grace; but never forgave Mr. Bryan for marrying her daughter or getting her pregnant.

Added to these concerns, the health of Lizzie's parents continued to decline. Her father suffered from periodic colds; her mother, from influenza and a uterine tumor. Because Mrs. Chester lived some distance from medical help, she described her symptoms to Lizzie, who in turn, conveyed them to her physician, Edwin S. Kellogg. The doctor attempted to prescribe medicines to curb the cancer and relieve the pain, among them Kali-Phosphorus, a potassium phosphate powder.

Lizzie's worries proved justified. Her father died in early 1892, and her mother lived only sixteen months longer.

Helena, May 14th, 1882

My dear Mother:

I cannot tell you of the weary, weary, days and nights I have spent during the last few months. Fortunately they are ended, and the dear babies are here. For they brought the love and welcome with them, though I had felt entirely unreconciled to the thought of such an addition to my cares. Even now it seems a weary task to get them safely started on life's voyage and my strength seems most inadequate to the task. You know I do not have much assistance in training the children. . . .

[Sept. 14, 1882]

After the Chinese boy came it was of course a little easier, but he was ignorant of every detail of housekeeping and needed some one with him constantly. Now he can wash the dishes, no small item in a family the size of ours, and though his dish towels are apt to be a little "off color" he does give us clean shining glass and silver and smooth plates and platters . . . and he does all the washing for the babies and when nothing else offers can take the little ones out for a ride. So you see "Ah Gim" is a useful member of our family, and as he is good natured and speaks very little English we cannot complain of either manners or morals. . . .

[Jan. 28th, 1883]

I sent away my Chinaman; . . . we could not afford to keep him for he wanted eight dollars per week. . . . We send out all our washing now, have a woman come in to sweep, scrub, and help with any extra work, and if we could only farm the babies out during meals, could get along very nicely. As it is we are not more tired than we were while we had more <u>help</u>? and have not one-half the worry. I felt as if the Chinaman was "making off" with something every time he left the house and his numerous visitors who might have slipped any number and quantity of things into their pockets or up their capacious sleeves. . . .

117

The Indian maid, Zillah, has been home on a visit for the last two or three days and I have missed her so much in the care of the babies. She will take them both and seating herself on the floor with them amuse them by the hour in such foolish innocent ways, ways only a child could devise or a baby enjoy. She does some things about the house, but nothing very nicely. Neatness and order are lacking in her composition but I may perhaps be able to instill them. She is strong, good natured and willing and loves me very devotedly. At her books she is very dull, and my patience sometimes "gives out," but she can tell now "how many are two and two" and read just a little better than when she came. . . .

[June 25th, '83]

I am so delighted at the thought that you are really coming at last that I have laughed and cried since the letter came and I fear am writing some what incoherently.

The fare between New York and Helena is about one hundred dollars, sleeping car section will be about thirty more, meals seventy five cents. After purchasing tickets, <u>through</u> to Helena you would not need more than one hundred dollars for all other expenses and this is money enough to carry about with one when traveling. . . . If you want a fast ride you can come over the Pennsylvania R.R. from N.Y. to Chicago in twenty-six hours; from Chicago to St. Paul is about twenty-four hours, and from St. P. to Helena two days.

It is a goodly sight to see the train coming in here every evening and we drive down almost every day. The depot is about 3/4 of a mile from our house. The children have not yet had a ride on the cars except Robbie who made friends with an engineer and rides on the iron horse.

Yours lovingly,
L.C. Fisk

[Northern Pacific tracks reached Helena in mid-June and Lizzie's parents arrived a month later. They stayed for two months then returned to Connecticut by first traveling west on the Northern Pacific, over Mullan Pass, to Garrison. There they caught the Montana Union south to Silver Bow (near Butte) where they transferred to the Utah and Northern which took them to Corinne, Utah, and the main line of the Union Pacific.]

My dear Mother:

After we left you on Monday we had time to walk over and inspect the [Gregson Hot] Springs near the depot. We were sorry you could not have gone with us to see this most curious formation. There are eight or ten boiling springs varying in temperature from eighty degrees to one hundred and ninety. The crater of one of them had been sounded to the depth of ninety feet. The water is strongly impregnated with iron and soda and in one place a mound about twenty feet high has been formed by the constant bubbling of the water and in the center of this, the open crater is fathomless.

A summerhouse with seats is built on the summit of the mound and the view from this spot is most beautiful. The whole valley, in this place nearly thirty miles wide, is spread out like a picture. The house, grounds, bath-rooms and everything about the place are kept with the most exquisite neatness, and we wondered that the place was not more widely known.

But we were warned by the smoke of the locomotive far away up the valley that we must descend from the heights, and soon we were steaming back to Deer Lodge where we stopped for supper and so had time to see the little town.

Arrived once more at the [Garrison] Junction, our time of waiting began, but we had a comfortable car, a good fire, books and knitting work and when all these failed took quite a comfortable nap. It was twelve o'clock, midnight, when our train arrived and half-past three when we reached Helena, and it is safe to say there was sufficient grumbling done on board the train to mar the pleasure of the whole [Henry] Villard party,[1] had they heard it. But we were only too glad to reach home at so early an hour, as the trains since that day have been from twelve to twenty-four hours behind time. . . .

We found everything all right at home and after a few hours sleep took up again our daily duties. But we do miss you so much. For the first few days, James and Florence traveled up stairs many times and to your room and would come down looking so disappointed.

With love from all,
L.C. Fisk

[Events in the Fisk family during 1884 remain obscure. No letters from 1884 survive in the Fisk papers. Lizzie was ill during a portion of the year, prompting Grace to return home from school in Minnesota. During this time, it is possible Lizzie wrote no letters. Any remaining correspondence from that year was lost before the papers were donated to the Montana Historical Society. Details of family life during this year emerge from subsequent letters and from scattered articles in the *Helena Herald*.]

Helena, Feb. 15th / 85

My dear Mother:

I have felt that if I could get through last week without another attack of the fever I should be far on the road to recovery; and I am sure I have not much more to dread from rheumatism since the weather for a week past has been very comfortable. . . .

Our young people were all excitement yesterday over St. Valentine's Day. . . . Grace received a beautiful valentine, satin, hand-painted, opening like a book, and having two landscapes which are frosted like some of the Christmas cards. And inside the box was a little gold nugget with a ring to attach it to pin or watch chain.

She. . . has received so much attention since she has been home. I shall really be glad on some accounts, when she goes back to school. She is prettier than ever this winter, so bright and fresh it does one good to look at her, and I don't wonder the boys like to take her out. I don't so much object to the school boys — her mates — but try to keep away the older ones. . . .

One of the boys brought her the card which was pinned to Con Murphy when he was hung — it has the skull and cross-bones and the magic figures 3-7-77. What did you think of the hanging? I have wondered how it would impress eastern people. . . .

> With love from all,
> L.C. Fisk

Boulder Springs,
June 17th, 1885

My dear Mother:

We left home yesterday morning, [and] took a coach over the mountains to Boulder City. . . . The [Hot Springs Resort] is quite comfortable and the baths delightful. We have a quiet room in a little cottage with baths attached, and can be by ourselves when we like. There are a good many children here and we are very glad we left ours at home. . . .

Friday morning

The place lies in Boulder Valley. At the back are high hills where are found the mineral springs which supply the water for the baths. These are so hot where they bubble from the ground that you cannot hold a

120

finger in them for an instant. The water is brought in large pipes to reservoirs where it is cooled sufficiently for use. There is a large swimming bath which people use as for surf bathing; swimming suits are furnished and boarders and both ladies and gentlemen sport in this and have "lots of fun.". . . .

In the building where we stay there are six bath rooms with large zinc tubs. These are intended more particularly for invalids as the temperature can be easily regulated. The water is soft and very pleasant to use and effects some wonderful cures in rheumatism, neuralgia and many other diseases. . . . In front of this house is another spring from which people are expected to drink "early and often."

The Hotel proper stands on higher ground, here we go for meals and to see the crowd when we are weary of our own society. In front of all these buildings lies the valley, at this point quite narrow but beautifully green and filled with wild flowers and singing birds. The hillsides, too, are covered with flowers. We gathered ten or twelve varieties in a short walk the evening of our arrival.

I send you a "Bitterroot" blossom,[2] one of the prettiest of the wild flowers. It comes out of the ground without leaf or anything green, just the stem with bud and flower. The blossoms close at night and open with the morning sun. The smaller flowers must be a wild phlox, I think. The ferns come from the hillside. . . .

[Helena, July 3rd, 1885]

You asked in one of your letters "Has Mary [Knipper] a beau?" [F]or a year past we have received frequent calls from Mr. [Clifford H.] Anderson who is . . . "a nice young man." He has been kind to us all in many ways but never showed Mary any particular attention till last spring.

His visits have been very frequent of late and while we were away at the Springs he asked Mary to marry him and they are now engaged. . . . I do like Mr. Anderson and am sure he will make a good husband. He went to Rob yesterday and told him of his proposal to Mary and hoped we would look favorably on his suit. We have, of course, no right to interfere in the matter as Mary is "of age" and so her own mistress. . . .

[July 31st, 1885]

Robbie went out with his Uncle Van this morning for a few days sport and to bring in a horse Rob has bought. Van has been traveling for the *Herald* this summer but has now purchased an interest in a little paper published at Townsend. . . . It is called the *Tranchant*. Van will take his family out there soon. . . .

121

Wagon Bridge in Prickley Pear Canyon near Helena. —Montana Historical Society

We went out last week for a little trip to the Prickley Pear Canyon [with] . . . Uncle Charlie and Mae. . . . We drove through to our destination, Lyon's Creek, the first day, and here . . . we camped. . . . It was a most delightful spot away up in the mountains. The air was odorous with pine balsam and the cleanest and coldest of mountains streams dashed over the rocks, in the shadow of overhanging willows. . . .

Bright and early the following morning Rob, Mae and I went fishing while Charlie mounted a horse and went to the very summit of the mountain in search of bear or deer. He was unsuccessful, and we caught only four fish. . . . In the afternoon we harnessed up and drove down into Prickley Pear Canyon where we caught a fine mess of fish. There we camped beside the river in the shadow of rocks three hundred feet in height and cooked the fish for our supper. I believe it was the best meal I ever ate.

Then in the moonlight we drove up the Canyon five miles . . . where we spent the night and the following day came home. . . . I had never really seen the Canyon since I came to Montana eighteen years ago, but it has lived in my memory as one of the most beautiful places I ever saw. And my second visit was not a disappointment, it was even more beautiful than I thought. The rock formations . . . tower . . . high and are worn by wind and storm into fantastic shapes [and] there is here an abundance of vegetation. Evergreens of different varieties seem growing from the very rocks, rose-bushes with their bright red berries are wreathed with the clematis with its feathery tassels, and many of the shrubs and bushes had been touched by the frost and donned their autumn robes. . . .

The clock is striking ten.

> With love,
> L..C. Fisk

Helena, Jan. 19th / 86

My dear Mother:

[O]ur plans for a New Year's reception . . . were carried out and proved a great success. . . . the button hole bouquets which were tied to a card containing a text of Scripture were very beautiful and the passage of Scripture seemed to fit every case. One poor old man came in there, a miserable drunkard, yet not wholly lost to every right feeling, for at the first kind word the tears streamed from his eyes and when I handed him his little flower he rose and left the table and the room.

Some of the young men went to look him up and found him in the hall weeping because "every one was so good to him." His text was, "For with the Lord there is mercy and with him there is plenteous redemption." Did ever a sinner need it more?

123

We had some beautiful little pledges printed, both the Liquor and Tobacco and procured many signatures especially among the young men and boys. . . .

Tomorrow the Chatauqua Circle meets and I must confess that I am not very well up in Roman History. I have done very little reading during two weeks past and that all after nine o'clock at night. And I do not remember as well as I used to do. . . .

[Jan. 24th, 1886]

I did not honor the Charity Ball with my presence. . . . Grace went for a little while in company with Mr. and Mrs. [Francis] Pope, but was home early. She is fond of dancing as all young people are though she has few opportunities to indulge her taste. . . .

We have a set of very fast young men in Helena but they learned some time ago that Grace could not go out with them, and do not annoy her by further invitations. I mean young men who belong to our best families like the Hauser's and the Knights, and who were Grace's schoolmates not long ago. . . .

I do not believe it is possible in these western towns to bring up a girl. . . . without making her feel that she is badly used. I should have said a pretty girl. Grace's associates have always been older than herself, she is more mature than many girls of eighteen, . . . very womanly and self-reliant. . . .

> With love from all,
> L.C. Fisk

Helena, March 1, 1888

My dear Mother:

I have a good deal of excitement of late [because of Mary Knipper's wedding] and have not slept as much as usual. . . . We were up betimes Wednesday morning for half past six comes very early nowadays. . . . The ceremony was soon over though it seemed very long and prosy and then came the breakfast. The first course was oranges, and the next fried oysters, rolls and coffee, the third cold roast turkey, stewed potatoes, poached eggs on toast. Before we had finished breakfast the carriages came and we hurried away to the depot. Robbie and Clarke climbed out on the porch roof and showered the party with rice as they passed out. . . .

We are invited to attend the wedding of the richest man in Montana tomorrow morning at nine o'clock. The reception is to be given afterward at the Cosmopolitan Hotel. The happy man is Tommy Cruse, an illiterate Irishman about sixty years of age. The bride elect is Miss Maggie Carter a modest young lady, well educated, about twenty-four.

She must be selling herself for his gold. How can a young girl so debase herself? To think of living with that rough, dirty old sinner.

Maggie Salisbury says he has "the dust of ages" laid up in the creases of his neck. She sits behind him in church and she out to know. I am not going to either wedding or reception. They shall never say I toadied to their money. . . .

[March 31, 1886]

This afternoon I attended the regular monthly meeting of the W.C.T.U. This temperance organization has been languishing, but just now a new interest seems to be awakened in the subject and the meeting today was well attended. . . .

The Union has under its auspices work for the children in "Bands of Hope," for the older boys in Cadets of Temperance, and for the young ladies another organization.

They are working everywhere to introduce Scientific Temperance instruction in the schools of the country and latest work is for Social Purity. . . . There is work too in the jails, prisons, alms-houses. Indeed this Women's Christian Temperance Union neglects no opportunity for doing good, no means toward hastening the day when all men shall know and love the Lord.

We have done so little here in Helena, have been so weak and discouraged and had so many enemies to fight. I do hope we shall now be able to accomplish more, for I never felt the need of temperance work so greatly as since the Cruse wedding. Just think of the boys who have grown up in our midst who were that day sent home to their mothers intoxicated. Think of the men who made beasts of themselves because the wine was free.

[Sept. 12th, 1886]

Our water troubles are a fruitful topic. . . . the worst story I heard in connection with the subject was that the boys used to go swimming in a small pond, the water from which flowed into the reservoir. They kept this up till the water smelled so badly even the boys could not endure it any longer and the long-suffering citizens of Helena drank that water.

We filter and boil all we drink or use for cooking. The city council declared that water a public nuisance and the reservoir has been thoroughly cleaned so we hope for an improvement. . . .

Your loving daughter,
L.C. Fisk

Helena, Nov. 4th, 1886

My dear Mother:

Florence has been sick for a week past with scarlet fever. . . . Where she contracted the fever will ever remain a mystery, for she never goes anywhere, but I think the germs must be floating around in the air since there are many cases in town. We are giving the other children medicine and hope they may escape. The yellow [quarantine] card on our porch tacked up by the city Marshall keeps callers away and we do not go out except for air so we are really having a nice quiet time. . . .

[Nov. 14th, 1886]

You are anxious for news of our scarlet fever patient and I rejoice to be able to tell you that she has entirely recovered. . . . she looks a little thin and pale, but . . . we watched her so carefully afterward during the critical time when she was in danger of taking cold that she has escaped all unpleasant after effects. . . .

I told the doctor I was not all anxious to have the card removed since the people we were really anxious to see came in spite of the card and those mere acquaintances who would come for a fashionable call, book agents, peddlers and tramps generally were kept out and I need not waste my time on them. He laughed and remarked he should not want one on his door.

You ask who is my new doctor? He is [E.S. Kellogg] a Yankee from Vermont, though he has lived west so long as to consider himself a western man. He is a scholar and a refined Christian gentleman. And better than all, he has almost cured me. There are days at a time when I forget all about my gout, and I do not look like the same person. The horrible ashen-hue is gone from my face and I am growing pink and rosy, "renewing my youth.". . .

I must say Good Bye.

L.C. Fisk

Helena, Nov. 28th, 1886

My dear Mother:

Did I write you of our visit to the "poor farm?" . . . I drove down taking [Rev. T.V.] Moore and Mrs. [Laura E.] Howey. We were not expected but were cordially welcomed and Mr. Moore held the first [Protestant] religious service ever given on the place. . . . We found old men and boys, middle-aged men and two women who listened gladly to the reading and singing. Tears stood in the eyes of several of the men as Mr. Moore spoke to them of the parable of the Prodigal Son. . . .

I went on Friday last, at Mrs. Howey's request, to see a boy who is in the jail here. He says cards have been his ruin, he was brought up to play and had an inherited taste for gambling. . . . In an evil moment he yielded to temptation and pawned a watch and chain not his own. A friend had given him the articles while under the influence of liquor. And now he is suffering the penalty of his crime. . . .

[Feb. 11, 1887]

Our poor committee has been kept busy. There are many cases of sickness and destitution. Men out of work and having no provision for "a rainy day." Mothers deserted, or robbed of the husband and farther by death, and in some cases having [large] families. . . . Indeed the only wealth these families possess consists of children. One poor woman, whose husband has recently died after a long illness which exhausted all their savings, and who has five little ones, the eldest seven years of age, said with tears in her eyes "I would live on one meal a day sooner than part with my children." . . .

Our W.C.T.U. work is not neglected or forgotten. . . . We have kept up the interest in the society, [and] . . . have a room of our own which we shall soon furnish and our plan is to make this the beginning of our House for working women, of which we have so long talked. There are often girls coming here in search of work who are friendless and who need some place where they can stay without going to a Hotel or public place. These girls sometimes fall into bad company and are ruined.

[Feb. 22nd, 1887]

You speak of the question before the Legislatures of the various states and territories in regard to the protection of young girls. This is W.C.T.U. work and our Union has not been behind in her duty. The first bill introduced in the House was in regard to Rape. This was passed early in the session though the age was cut down from eighteen to fifteen years. In company with Mrs. Howey, I went before the Council Committee to whom this bill was referred. . . .

I cannot tell you how hard it was to go before this committee one of whom was [a] <u>cranky bachelor</u> and talk about these things. But I kept thinking of the two girls, school mates of Grace's, and younger than she is, who have been led away and ruined and are now leading lives of shame. And so for them and thousands of others like them I tried to be brave.

Judge [Cornelius] Hedges drew up a bill against seduction which passed the Council but was presented by the House Committee with the recommendation that it do not pass, which kills it, I suppose.[3] . . .

Yours lovingly,
L.C. Fisk

My dear Mother:

When I wrote you last I was waiting for [housekeeper] No. 3. She made her appearance the next evening and commenced work Tuesday morning. She claimed to have had "a deal of experience" and to understand all kinds of cooking, but regaled us with our sour bread and like delicacies. Roasts with a nice brown gravy had never entered into her idea of cookery. When she saw a steak brought in the house for dinner she said with such an air of assurance, "You want your steak fried." I told her "No, we always broil it." Then she inquired, "How long does it take to do that, you said boil it was it?"

I determined to be very patient and teach her but found she only cared to stay a month, to earn a little spending money. . . . So Rob prevailed on No. 2 to come back. She is a good girl, but so very slow, and could not cook or rather bake any thing eatable. . . . Saturday evening I received a letter from Rica [No. 1] saying her husband was compelled to be away and she would come back to me for a couple of months. I answered the letter before I slept and told her I should be delighted to have her back, and Tuesday evening she returned "bag and baggage," so I am at rest again for two months. . . .

[Oct. 16th, 1887]

I suppose you read of Cardinal [James] Gibbon's visit to Helena, reception &c. Well, Grace and I attended. . . . After I had been presented (I did not kiss the cardinal's ring which had been blessed by the Pope) Mr. [J.D.] Curtis brought a chair and seated me at the C.'s left hand and I had the pleasure of talking with him for nearly a half an hour, and better still of seeing the others who were presented and witnessing the awe of reverence with which the Catholics regarded him. . . .

There is one gentleman here, Mr. J.C. Curtin, who is noted for his excessive politeness. His stereotype expression when one visits his business house is "Call again, gentleman, call again," with a bow, a smile, and much rubbing of hands. "They say" that when a runaway occurred on Main Street some years ago, and the horses came crashing into Mr. Curtin's store he even preserved his usual serenity and as the horses were extricated from the midst of the hardware and led out he uttered the stereotyped "Call again." But even he could not open his lips before the Cardinal.

A number of prominent Southern gentlemen went up to pay their respects, among whom was Governor [Preston H.] Leslie, and the Reverend gentleman told them one of [James G.] Blaine's stories about "unreconstructed rebels" and I suppose thought they could not appreciate a good story because they could not see the fun in that. Take it all in all 'twas a pleasant half hour, and I rather admire Cardinals. . . .

Last evening I attended the opening meeting of the Presbytery now in session in this city. This morning also attended church and the two sermons have used me up completely. I told Rob when I came home last evening that if all the brains of the members of the Presbytery were simmered together <u>one</u> average brain would be the result. Since listening to the sermon this morning I am in doubt whether,

> "Set them to simmer and take off the scum
> An average brain would be 'the residuim. . . .'"

The children have all been vaccinated during the past week, so we are looking for sore arms. Asa's is already a good deal inflamed. . . .

[Apr. 11th, 1888]

[Buying a house] lost its interest for Grace when she learned that, being a minor, she could not legally hold land or other property. And you, my dear mother, would be no better off, for after residing upon your land and going through all necessary formalities it would belong not to you but to your husband. Women <u>do</u> have a hard time in this world, don't they?

Do not think Grace is idling at home. She has painted and sold several pictures, realizing about one hundred dollars for them. She is making boxes for a candy factory, and makes and trims bonnets for the family and all her friends. I have advised her to learn to set type but no favorable time has yet presented itself. . . .

Goodnight, with much love,
L.C. Fisk

Helena, June 10th, 1888

My dear Mother:

I should have written you a week ago, but did not find time. When Rob and Grace got away [for a trip to California], I was pretty well tired out. . . . Then I was without help for several days and during the interval the house was entered by burglars. . . . I had been sleeping down stairs all alone, too, but last Thursday evening I got very nervous after reading of several houses which had been entered and I went up stairs with the children and locked myself safely in.

We heard not a sound but when I came down stairs in the morning such a sight as met my eyes. My writing desk lay in the middle of the dining room floor, papers scattered all about. Every bureau drawer had been ransacked and the contents strewn over the floor. Even the medicine case had been opened and examined, dresses were taken down from the wardrobe, the shoe bag searched and a pair of new kid shoes which I had worn only twice were taken; also a pair of new gloves from the glove box.

But the greatest find was a box of jewelry which contained my opal ring and three bracelets, a pair of sleeve buttons and I do not remember how many other things. There were a half dozen little boxes and cases which had once contained rings or other articles of jewelry but were now empty and I like to think of the disappointment of the fellows as they opened one after another, only to be disappointed. . . .

The men simply took the screen from the pantry window and set it carefully down. Nothing was broken, no silver taken though there were pounds of it in the kitchen cupboard. I was so thankful to escape thus easily. I must have felt a premonition of their coming for I had hidden my purse and three gold pins which were on the cushion in the bedroom and worn my gold hair pin up stairs. . . .

I have been dreadfully nervous over the affair and did not sleep till daylight, but last night did better and have taken a good nap today so I am ready for whatever may happen next. . . .

[October 3, 1888]

Rob and I drove down in the valley tonight to see about ranching one of our cows for the winter. Returning we drove up Main Street and Broadway. One needs to see the city at night to realize how it is growing and what a busy place it has become. Electric lights in every direction, street cars running every fifteen minutes, the walks filled with a hurrying crowd; a band playing in the distance and near at hand the harsh voices of Capt. Sharp and Cadet Nelson on the Salvation Army. I thought of you tonight and wished you might look upon the motley throng. . . .

Your loving daughter,
L.C. Fisk

Helena, Nov. 11th, 1888

My dear Mother:

Ought not the glorious election news to make every one feel good?. . . Our Democratic friends bet heavily and lost piles of money. I do not approve of betting, but I am so glad they lost for their success of four years ago had made them so confident and exceedingly disagreeable. . . Montana will surely be admitted as a state at the next session of Congress, a Republican state with a majority of five thousand to start with.

It does me lots of good to think the Democratic carpet baggers and office holders must go. We all rejoice, too, that Montana could not be bought with Mr. [William A.] Clark's money bags. It is estimated that

130

he spent one hundred thousand dollars on the election, only to be defeated. . . .

The *Record* was started last fall as a daily paper. Its original owners soon exhausted their capital and were glad to dispose of their mortgages to Mr. [Russell B.] Harrison or his representatives. It is to be the administration organ, I suppose, though the appointment of territorial officials for the balance of the year will determine whether the [James G.] Blaine or [Benjamin] Harrison faction is to control Montana for the next few months. . . .

Russell B. is not remarkable for anything except his egotism and vanity. Until his father's nomination, was liked by few, and was spoken of with derision by almost every one. In business ventures in Montana he has failed. How much of his "pa's" salary will go to maintain the new organ has not yet been divulged. He will not be troubled to know <u>what to do with the surplus</u> of his own income, at all events.

The establishment of a new paper cannot fail to "injure the *Herald*." It divides patronage, if it does no more. Three daily papers in a city of this size cannot be well sustained, and while the *Herald* is run to pay expenses, the others are really brighter and more newsy and are trying to run the *Herald* out. . . .[4]

Accept love from all,
L.C. Fisk

Helena, Mch. 25th, 1889

My dear Mother:

Jamie met with an accident [last week] which might have been quite serious, but one of those good angels who watch over the little ones must have been near him. . . . [The housekeeper] came in bringing poor Jamie, with eyelashes and eyebrows burnt away, his whole face and one hand looking as if it was ready to blister. He and Eddie Pope had found two shot-gun shells out doors somewhere and cut them open, poured the powder on the porch and touched it off with a match. We could not tell at first whether his eyes were injured or not, and I feared he had inhaled the powder and smoke as he was sick at his stomach. I used everything I could think of to relieve the pain till the doctor could be found, but it seemed as if he would have convulsions he suffered so. It was not two minutes after the doctor applied his remedies before the child was perfectly easy. He used a spray of ether and then applied a preparation of peppermint with a little brush. We kept Jamie indoors for several days, used Cantharis Cerate and Cosmoline[5] and his skin now is pretty as ever. We think he even looks better, for his freckles are gone. . . . Even Jamie's stockings and the front of his shirt were scorched but fortunately his clothing was woolen.

[June 30th, 1889]

The Sunday finds us again at home after a pleasant trip to Missoula. . . . All the way to Missoula we follow clear mountain streams, through beautiful fertile valleys surrounded by lofty, heavily-wooded mountains. Missoula is a charming little city of about three thousand inhabitants. every attention was showed the members of the Press Association and their families.

The fruit and flowers growing so luxuriantly in the gardens of the city were our especial admiration. You can fancy the delight of the little ones in being able for the first time to climb a cherry tree and gather the fruit. They also saw strawberries, raspberries, blackberries, gooseberries and currants growing and were allowed to help themselves. Fruit trees were so heavily laden their branches were held up by strong timbers, apples, pears, plums, promising an abundant harvest. Grape vines with fruit slowly maturing and every where a wealth of roses, climbing over trellises made the air sweet. . . .

[July 7th, 1889]

Like you, I wonder how ladies find time for so many societies. Though a member of the W.C.T.U. I never attend the meetings. They have for a long time been held on Saturday afternoon, a time when I cannot well leave home. While I approve the temperance and reformatory work of the organization, I do object very strongly to the action of some of its leaders in attempting to commit the members to the third party movement. . . .

It may be right for women who have no children and few home cares to attend meetings constantly and work for the public. Those who have families certainly cannot do it.

The Fourth was a great success. . . . But for the sad accident in the evening, the day would have been perfect.[6] . . .The Yaeger boys have been here so much and were such nice boys they seemed very near to me and so when Asa and Clarke came home with the sad story I went down and helped in caring for the poor boy. As we washed and dressed him for the last time the thought was ever with me, "If one of my own boys had met this sad fate," for they were there in the throng and exposed to the same danger.

Both came home with tears streaming and Asa said "I never want to go any where again." Their few fireworks were put away, and they have had not heart to touch them since. I have always been so anxious about the children on the Fourth and when the city prohibited the sending off of fireworks within the fire limits I thought the little ones would all be safe. . . . The little boy was one of the *Herald* carriers, a boy universally loved. . . .

I am forgetting all about the weather and it really is entitled to a separate chapter. The forest fires are raging all about us, darkening the air with smoke and almost obscuring the sun. For two evenings past we have needed to light the lamps at six o'clock. Hundreds and perhaps thousands of cords of wood have been destroyed and all our beautiful forests are falling before the general destruction, . . . and our only hope seems in a heavy rain which we scarcely dare hope or expect, at this season of the year. . . .

> Yours with love,
> L.C. Fisk

[Preparatory to statehood, a Constitutional Convention met in Helena during July and August of 1889, drafting a document which the electorate approved in November. Unresolved, however, was the partisan controversy which continued to split Montana.]

Helena, Aug. 11th, 1889

My dear Mother:

Helena has been excited during the past week over the debates on the capital question in the [Constitutional] convention. The amount of venom and spite toward Helena displayed by the members from other parts of the Territory is something unaccountable. When one considers how these members are treated, dined and feted and transported from one point of interest to another, and then they turn about and vent all their corked up bile and bitterness on the people who have treated them so kindly. . . .

[Jan. 8th, 1890]

Mrs. and Miss [Wilbur F.] Sanders called [last evening]. . . . Mrs. S. has decided to go with her husband to Washington, for the Col. has at last reached the summit of his ambition and is to represent his State at the National Capital, if the U.S. Senate so decides.[7] He is wise to take his wife with him for she is discreet and polite and has done much to bring about his election and will help him there. . . . The situation of affairs would be amusing were it not so much to be regretted that Montana has made such a record for herself at the very beginning of Statehood. . . .

133

[Jan. 26th, 1890]

Uncle Van was brought to town about the time I wrote you last, very low from dropsey. He has been drinking <u>hard</u> for more than a year and this seemed to be almost the end. He was dreadfully bloated, was helpless and the disease was advancing so rapidly it seemed almost to have reached his heart. But he was placed in [the] Hospital, Dr. Kellogg took him in charge, after treating him several days tapped him and relieved the immediate danger. Whether he will ever be well enough to leave the Hospital we cannot tell but he is much more comfortable. . . .

[Feb. 23rd, 1890]

We stayed with [Van] quite a time, read to him and asked him if I might send a clergyman to see him. He was willing and glad to see the Episcopal minister [Rev. R.P. Eubanks] who is accustomed to hold service at Townsend. [He has] been very kind and [has] been much with Van who was last week baptized. . . .

The expense of keeping him in the Hospital is very heavy, the man who waits on him receives $18.00 per week, and all this his brothers do for him. I do not complain but such things are not right, for a man who has a family of his own to support. . . .

Robbie has just come in and says it is nineteen degrees below zero at the Merchants [Hotel] now, not yet nine o'clock. I am so tired of this intense cold. It is wearing to the nerves, keeping one strung up to highest tension. Then we have <u>five</u> fires running all the time and it is all one can do to run from stove to stove and keep the house warm. Even then we traverse cold halls that almost take one's breath away, and the house is strewn with dirt and bits of bark from end to end. I do hope for some better arrangement before another winter. [A] new house seems to me a necessity. If I could only make Rob look at it in that light, but I do not despair of talking him over. . . .

[March 11th, 1890]

Papa and I are having a good many differences of opinion in regard to building. He did not like the lots I selected and had an option on, so I gave them up. I have never dared discuss the plan with him. I was very bad, I suppose, but I finally told him when he asked how I proposed to maintain a more expensive house, if he would let his brothers take care of themselves he would be able to do more for his own family. I do get indignant when I think of it, how hard I work and try to economize and he throws away hundreds of dollars in that way every year. He says what would you have me do? Send them to the poor house? But I tell him if he had made them understand twenty years ago they must support themselves they would not look to him now. . . .

134

We attended the Opera last night, saw Faust. Miss [Emma] Juch has a sweet, true voice but I was a little disappointed in her. She has a broad Dutch face, and a broad, Dutch figure. The singers are nearly all foreigners and though they sang in English they might just as well have used their native tongues for all any one could understand. One man sang "Et es the geeft of my seester!" good English! . . .

[April 15, 1890]

Van is a great care and a constant worry. . . . His business in Townsend was closed up, the little material he had packed away. His brothers had paid his workmen, bought his paper and other stock, paid rent, meat bills and milk bills, so it was a relief to them when the paper was suspended. . . . .

[Apr. 28th, 1890]

Uncle Van died on Saturday, the 19th. . . . It was a relief to every one when his sufferings were at last over. He was buried from the Episcopal church, in which he was baptized during his last illness. The service was beautiful.

The spring has at last come to Montana. For a week past the days have been warm, bright and sunny. The robins are singing, trees are budding and the lawns are looking beautifully. . . .

All send love.

Your daughter,
L.C. Fisk

Helena, June 15th, 1890

My dear Mother:

Grace, Asa, Jamie and Florence are quite taken up with rehearsals for the operetta of "Red Riding Hood" in which they take part. Grace and Asa are among the soloists. Florence is a blue bell and Jamie sings in the boy's chorus. . . .

Broadwater Plunge is the fashionable resort just now for Helena people and their visitors. Our boys do go along with others and I do not know that there is any greater objection to bathing there than to surf bathing. The suits are like those worn at the sea side and the diving and swimming are certainly desirable accomplishments for a boy. I do not like or allow our boys to go in oftener than once a week, usually on Saturday. . . .

Grace says tell Grandma to please spell Mr. [Walter S.] Kelley's name with two "e's." He is very particular about that, says he is not Irish but Scotch. No, I don't think the piano was a reward for not

135

marrying Mr. K. but rather "or who?" That is, it was the general principle, the being willing to defend such matters. You know if girls and boys can once be brought safely past the foolish age they are then willing to wait till their own characters are developed and they can choose wisely their future life companions. It requires some diplomacy, much tact and more patience to guide them through this critical period. I hope mine will hold out. . . .

[Sept. 7th, 1890]

I wish any woman who imagines it easier to bring up a family of children in the west than at the east might have her lot cast in Helena for a time, and I suppose this is no worse than other western cities. We have today in Helena licensed gambling houses to say nothing of the saloons open all the time. The Coliseum is a low theatre,[8] I hardly know how to describe it where girls serve the drinks in booths and lure men in and tonight, to crown all, we have at the [Ming] Opera House a wrestling match. . . .

On Tuesday afternoon I had a long talk with [Grace]. I used every argument I could think of and I had carefully considered the matter for days. I told her I did not see how she could ever be happy with a man [Hardy Bryan] who had influenced her to treat her mother unkindly, showed her how dictatorial and overbearing he had proved himself, told her all my fears for her future happiness. Such an argument as I made would have carried a jury but had little effect on her. . . .

Last evening we went out to the Broadwater for a Concert. Mr. B. sat down beside Grace, not sat down, he always lounges,, and puffed his cigar smoke in her face and dropped the ashes on her dress. It is not strange she cannot see. . . . What Grace will do this winter I do not see. She cannot afford to go on with her painting, she has spent a hundred dollars in china painting this summer. She cares very little for music, she can't loaf and read novels all the time. . . .

[Sept. 14th, 1890]

Grace . . . is going on with the preparations for her marriage and the date now fixed is the 8th of Oct. Mr. B. was very impudent and declared it should take place . . . the 17th of this month. I said "it cannot." I will not take one stitch or do one thing to help for any such date as that nor shall the marriage take place at home at that time. They both understand how we feel about it. . . .

Clarke writes me he likes his school [Howard Military Academy in Ogden, Utah]. . . . He is a good, honest boy as this fall shows, has never given me an hour's anxiety. . . .

Robbie is bright and wide awake, known and liked by everybody. Just now he is much interested in the Fire Department, turns out to

136

every fire, is a volunteer fireman, likes it for the excitement of the thing. He might choose a more objectionable way to work off his surplus energy, and will get over this after a time. . . .

I think I shall put Florence in a Convent when she is sixteen and keep her there till she is twenty-five if she [exhibits] a taste for frivolity. You may be assured I shall do my best to keep her in the right way. . . .

[Sept. 23, 1890]

I am glad you sent me Grace's letter as I shall reply to it separately and show my answer to her. . . . I do not feel that I have ever neglected home or home duties for any outside work or pleasure. I cannot live wholly within that narrow circle, nor do I think it any woman's duty to do so. There have been many years of my married life when the children were small that I could not get away from them and then I stayed at home. But I think every mother should have hours of rest and relaxation, of freedom from care, and she must find it outside the home. She has more strength and patience, is better fitted to care for her little ones, if she can sometimes get away from them and they appreciate her far more. In the light of recent events I am sure it is a mistake to deny oneself for the children. . .

The time has passed when I shall attempt to smooth over and make the best of things when I shall deny myself many things I need. I propose to have my turn at what ever pleasure or profit I can lay hold of, for life is fast passing away and all my strength is spent for others.

The first of these reforms comes in the shape of a new bath room and water closet connected with our bedroom, which was commenced yesterday. We will try to be a little more comfortable this winter.

With much love,
L.C. Fisk

[Grace and Hardy Bryan married October 1. While Lizzie did some of the sewing and preparation for the wedding she and Robert did not attend.]

Helena, Nov. 16, 1890

My dear Mother:

R.E., D.W., and A.J. [Fisk] are not equal owners in the *Herald*. Rob owns half, the others each a quarter interest which he gave them. . . . I sometimes think the brothers would have been wise to accept the offer made them for the *Herald* last Summer, $75,000. This did not include the building which they could have rented and the money invested in other buildings to rent would bring in much larger income than it now does. But they wanted more, and may not soon have another offer. . . .

You ask if Grace is happy. I should not be likely to know it if she were not. She seems to live in a whirl, but has taken up with a set we did not receive or encourage at home. . . . Some of my friends who know of the circumstance of her marriage have not called [on Grace] because as one of them said "she has not honored you after all you have done for her." These were friends who have been much in our home and know of what they are talking. . . .

[Feb. 22nd, 1891]

Our legislature at last got down to business . . . . but there was so little time that not much needed legislation will be accomplished. . . . There is one class of legislation I would like to see attempted and carried, one which would give employers some rights. Now everything is in the hands of the laborer. In the printing business, for instance, the employees dictate, through their union, the number of hours worked, the pay for the same, who shall be employed and what shall be printed. And does the mistress fare much better at the hands of her maid servant? . . . I do everything outside the kitchen. . . .

[Mch. 8th, 1891]

We have such good news from Clarke. He has been made a Sergeant and [his] Professor writes us, "He is making considerable progress in his studies. His deportment is in every way satisfactory and I consider your son to be one of the best cadet officers we have. He is thoroughly reliable and attends strictly to his business." . . . Clarke's marks for the last Half Quarter were two 90's, the highest marks given, in Algebra and Book-keeping. . . .

[Mch. 29th, 1891]

Rob told me yesterday noon some gentleman had called upon him in the morning asking if I would permit my name to be used as a candidate for school trustee. I said "No, I thank you," most emphatically. I have all the duties I can attend to. The work among the poor which is constantly growing in interest and magnitude demands all the time and strength I can spare from home. This work I love and would not willingly give up.

I at last succeeded in obtaining an interview with Dr. Kellogg [about your illness] and as a result I send you tomorrow a package of medicine. The Kali-Phosphorus will, he thinks, help you at once. He says you should have local treatment but as this is impossible, he sends the

138

Boracic Acid to be used with hot water as a [douche]. Of the medicines, the Kali regulates the mucus secretions, the Phosphorus controls hemorrhages. There must be a relaxed condition of the neck and wall of the arteries, this will be helped by the remedies. The doctor said you needed not so much a general tonic as one which would act directly upon the affected parts. And you will experience no griping or unpleasant effects. I hope you will be benefitted. . . .

All are well and unite with me in much love.

Your daughter,
L.C. Fisk

Helena, Apr. 26th, 1891

My dear Mother:

Rob came home just before Sunday school time and proposed that we all go out to Lenox to call on the Andersons.[9] So we took the 4:30 [street] car at the corner of Rodney and Fifth and paid a visit to this new suburb. . . .

Some twelve or fifteen houses, all modern in style and quite imposing, have been built since that time, and the streets graded and much work accomplished. But a great deal still remains to be done before one can live comfortably. No grass, no trees, no walks, but dust or mud. I am more and more convinced that I do not care for a suburban residence. . . .

Mary Anderson has a nice house, the lower rooms finished in hard wood. There are pretty fire-places, nice closets and bath room, linen closet, a side board, built in, as also a book case. As the place cost about six thousand dollars and the first house they built is not yet paid for, it will be some time before they get "out of the woods." I think Mr. Anderson has gone into it for a speculation and will sell if he can do so advantageously and the monthly payments he can look upon as house rent. All the houses in Lenox are built in this way and it is quite possible some of them will change hands a good many times. . . .

[May 18th, 1891]

You ask about Grace. She is as well as could be expected for the thing happened which was to have been expected and she will soon be a mother, just as soon as possible I think. She does not go out much except to ride [which] has been a great comfort and source of pleasure to her. . . . I have never had any talk with her on the subject. At first I felt so badly about it I could not, and I have waited for her to broach the subject. If she could only have waited a reasonable time. Of course I do not feel any more kindly toward Mr. Bryan, as I realize that this all comes from allowing him to have his own selfish, hasty way. But I won't talk about it. . . .

June 15th, 1891]

I spoke to [Dr. Kellogg] about your bill and he said "Tell her we charge $10.00 for a prescription here," and laughed. Rob settled with him the first of the month for the quarter. The whole bill was $10.00. I suppose yours was $2.00 with possibly .50 more for the Kali-Phos. So you need not worry about that, as it is paid. I asked him about tonics and told him what you had said about Iron and Quinine. He said, "Don't take them. They will do no good. Keep on with the Kali-Phos., &c." . . .

Times are hard, work scarce, the town has been overbuilt, vacant homes on every side. We hear of hundreds and even thousands of idle men in Butte and Anaconda. And yet wages do not come down! Many will beg or starve rather than work for a cent less than they have been accustomed to earn. I pay a woman who cleans house for me $2.00 a day, a man has $2.50 or more. Provisions of all kinds, except meat, are reasonably low. . . .

With love,
L.C. Fisk

Helena, Sept. 14th, 1891

My dear Mother:

Have I ever told you that we are using electric lights all through the house? We had the house wired about the first of July and though our chandeliers have not come yet we are very brilliant with the one light in each room. No more slopping of coal oil, cleaning of lamps or breaking of chimneys. No heat or smoke, but a clear, steady light, just by turning a screw. Now if I only had a heater and could dispense with wood stoves I should be well pleased.

[Nov. 1st, 1891]

We have been enjoying some most delicious venison since Robbie's return [from a hunting trip] and are to have some dried elk meat. Robbie is to commence work in the *Herald* Office tomorrow, is to try his hand at telegraph editing and proof reading and so save his papa's eyes. Rob, the elder, has lately taken to wearing glasses when he has so much reading. The short winter days with so much artificial light are especially trying. . . .

[Dec. 29th, 1891]

Our children passed pleasantly as could have been expected. We had twenty at dinner including the baby, and twenty-five for the tree. Auntie Mae and all the family were up, the Anderson's, Grace and her family, and eight of us. . . .

140

Florence Fisk in the yard at 319 North Rodney, 1898. —Montana Historical Society

We sat down at four o'clock at two tables. . . . As soon as the Andersons came we lit the tree using electric lights. The effect was good and we had no candles to watch and no wax drippings to clear from the carpet or gifts. We had many little and pretty things upon the tree as there were so many to be remembered. . . .

I wish you could have seen the little ones. They are beautiful children and were so happy. Grace's baby had his mouth in a round O all the time till he grew sleepy and tired. . . . How I wish you could have been here in person and enjoyed it with us. . . .

No more tonight except love,
L.C. Fisk

Don't get the "grippe."

---

[1] Henry Villard, President of the Northern Pacific at the time of its completion, held a grand "Last Spike" ceremony on September 8. For the occasion, Villard and the N.P. assembled four trains of guests and dignitaries, headed by former President Ulysses S. Grant and British Under Secretary Lord Carrington. The "Villard Party" enjoyed lavish hospitality and frequent celebrations all along the railroad's route, disrupting normal train transportation.

[2] *Lewisia redivia*, which became Montana's state flower in 1895.

[3] The bill did pass, giving unmarried women or the parents of minors the right to sue for damages in case of seduction.

[4] The *Helend Record* began publication as a weekly on March 25, 1888, converting to a daily September 7, 1888. On March 19, 1889, this morning, Republican newspaper changed its name to *The Helena Journal*. It continued under that masthead until the corporation became bankrupt November 9, 1892 and ceased publication. Russell B. Harrison, son of President Bejamin Harrison, headed the Journal Publishing Company, also serving as secretary for the Territorial Board of Stock Commissioners and the Montana Stock Growers Association. Harrison's paper gave Helena two morning dailies -- the *Republican Journal* and the *Democratic Independent.*. The *Republican Herald* was an evening paper. Apart from the fiscal implications of divided Republican patronage (printing contracts, etc.) Lizzie was probably justified in her concern that the general public would be divided. Circulation figures for the papers are not available, but the *Herald* format had changed little since the 1860s, with heavy combinations of advertising and news. The *Journal* and the *Independent* used more features and illustrations.

[5] Cantharis Cerate was a wax salve of dried beetles, used as a counterirritant. Cosmoline was a trade name for a petroleum base salve.

[6] Lancelot (Lancey) D. Yeager, son of music teacher Henry C. Yeager, died instantly the night of July 4th, when struck by a carelessly placed skyrocket, which ignited and flew into the crowd assembled to watch the firework display.

[7] Partisan accusations of voting fraud, particulary in Precinct 34, Silver Bow County, split the first session of the state Legislative Assembly in 1889-1890. Prior to direct election in 1913, state legislatures selected U.S. Senators and when the task came before Montana's divided body, the Democrats selected William A. Clark and Martin Maginnis, while the Republicans nominated Wilbur F. Sanders and Thomas C. Power. the U.S. Senate resolved the issue April 16, 1890, recognizing the credentials of Sanders and Power, sending the Democrats back to Montana.

[8] The Coliseum Theater on Wood Street, typified variety theaters of the era. Josephine Hensley, the Coliseum's proprietor, had been, successively, a Helena prostitute, madam and dance hall owner since 1867.

[9] Clifford Anderson, then manager of the insurance department of the Wallace and Thornburgh Real Estate Agency, lived on Jerome Place in the Lenox Addition. This subdivision lay about one and one half miles east of Helena's downtown area. In an effort to attract customers to the delight of "country" living, developers built large homes and constructed a street railway line to connect the addition with the business district.

Robert E. Fisk. —Montana Historical Society

My Dear Mother — 1892 - 1893

We are poor indeed since we have no longer
a father and grandfather to pray for us.

(Jan. 12, 1892)

Issac Chester died at his home in Vernon Center, Connecticut on January 6, 1892, of the grippe — influenza. He was 78 years of age. Mrs. Chester, recovering from the same illness as well as other physical ailments, did not attend her husband's funeral. Lizzie and Robert did not learn of the death until after the burial. They both considered it proper to mourn a full year and as a result, did not celebrate their twenty-fifth wedding anniversary March 21, 1892.

Lizzie encouraged her mother to visit or live in Helena and Mrs. Chester finally consented to come during the spring or summer of 1893. Her health did not improve sufficiently to allow it, however. Dr. Kellogg continued to provide medications and Lizzie always provided encouragement.

Another death caught Lizzie's attention and that of all Montana. Charles A. Broadwater died unexpectedly on May 24, 1892, at the age of 52. His extensive fortune and business investments in Montana included merchandising, real estate, railroad construction, plus the hotel and hot springs resort west of Helena which bore his name. Broadwater's funeral was the largest ever held in Helena.

Montana experienced economic depression in the early 1890s, caused in part by uncertainties regarding the future of silver in the United States monetary system. The question nagged Helena and much of the West. It worsened in what became known as the Panic of 1893, when the federal government ceased purchasing silver altogether. As a result of the downturn in 1892, but more directly because Benjamin Harrison lost the November election to Democrat Grover Cleveland, the *Helena Journal* ceased publication. Lizzie expressed understandable delight.

Hardy Bryan changed jobs and residences yet another time during the spring of 1892. He became a bookkeeper for the Helena Electric Railway Company and moved his family to the west side of town, some distance from the Fisk home. Other family members experienced trying times as well. Dan Fisk's father-in-law, City Treasurer James B. Walker, faced accusations of malfeasance in office for the loss of $6000 in city funds. Although never convicted of wrongdoing, the incident ruined his career. Lizzie felt Walker's affinity for liquor contributed to the problem.

Clarke continued his studies at C.L. Howard's military academy in Ogden and graduated in June of 1892. Lizzie attended the ceremony and recorded the vicissitudes of rail travel on her return. During September of the same year Robert took Jamie and journeyed to Washington, D.C., for the national G.A.R. convention. Back east, they visited Mrs. Chester in Connecticut and Fisk relatives in Minnesota.

Lizzie took advantage of Robert's absence to undertake a major home improvement project. Convinced that Robert would never agree to buy a new house, Lizzie had a modern coal furnace installed in their exisiting one. The idea of replacing five wood stoves with a single furnace pleased her. Even Robert agreed to the convenience once the system was operational.

Montana's legislative assembly met in Helena during the winter of 1893, and Lizzie recorded its activities. A major controversy developed over selection of a U.S. Senator to replace Wilbur F. Sanders. The issue involved more than partisan politics. Copper magnate William A. Clark continued to aspire to national office. Both Clark and rival Marcus Daly, of the Anaconda Copper Company, used the senate seat and the legislature as forums for their personal ambitions and animosities. Money proved no object as the "War of the Copper Kings" raged until Daly's death in 1900.

On March 14, 1893, Lizzie received a telegram saying her mother was seriously ill. She left Helena the same day for Vernon Center. Azuba Chester died a month later. May 10th, Lizzie returned home after settling her mother's estate. Among the items she brought back were the letters she had written over the past twenty-five years. In a very real sense they were a book; a chronicle of Lizzie and her family; a history of Helena, of Montana, and of the western frontier.

Helena, Jan. 12th, 1892

My dear Mother:

What can I say! Less than two hours ago came the letter telling me that dear father had passed away. Hearing nothing from day to day I had thought all danger must be passed and you were both recovering. I am simply overwhelmed. Rob said each day "They must be better or you would hear," and now to think I shall never see him again. Jamie said "We ought to have gone last June. Now Granpa is dead and I don't remember him at all." . . .

My mind goes back to our last parting when you said "You will probably never see your father again," and still farther back to the good bye of '76 and the psalm father read that last morning. It was the 91st and I remember how his voice broke in both chapter and prayer for the little ones starting out on the long journey. We are poor indeed since we have no longer a father and grandfather to pray for us. . . .

146

Evening

So many kind friends have called this afternoon. To all sorrow has come and such sympathy is precious. Grace brought the baby up. He is a dear little comforter. . . .

With prayer that God will comfort and keep you.

> Your loving daughter,
> L.C. Fisk

Helena, Feb. 15th, 1892

My dear Mother:

The children are very glad to receive a letter from Grandma once more. . . . I wish you would carefully consider the matter of coming to us. . . . If the season is a prosperous one and the projected railways and public buildings are brought to Helena, I hope we may be able to dispose of our place advantageously and get a larger, better house with modern methods of heating. . . .

After waiting these many years, . . . I have at last decided to take a letter from the Presbyterian church and go where I belong, to the Congregational. Have attended there regularly . . . and now take the children and remain to Sunday School, which is at the close of morning service. They all like it even Asa says, "that is a dandy class," and we feel settled and that we belong somewhere. . . .

Next Thursday will be my birthday — forty-six — I really begin to feel old, though I am much better this winter than a year ago. My domestic is the best I have had in a long time and I am relieved of much care in that direction. . . . I find plenty of work to keep me busy, so many boys and girls to sew and knit and mend for, have been helping Grace on the baby's short clothes. . . .

[March 7th, '92]

I have done so little writing this winter that my hand soon cramps when I attempt to write and my characters become very irregular. I have had no outside work, no books to keep as Sec. or Treas., no reports to make out or business letters to write. As a result have accomplished a good deal of knitting and reading. . . . After many weeks I finished [Victor Hugo's] Les Miserables and I did enjoy it so much. As a rule French novels are forbidden books, but this is so grand, so thrilling in passage. Sometimes I found myself holding my breath, scarcely daring to read further, yet unwilling to lay the book aside. . . .

I sympathize with your loving for fish. We have salt mackerel for breakfast once a week and codfish once. But our markets are filled, especially during the Lenten season, with fish from both oceans, lakes and rivers. But Rob does not seem to care for these and brings home

147

meat, meat, meat, day after day. Just now eggs are plentiful and quite reasonable, only thirty cents [a dozen], so we have them almost every morning.

[Mar. 14th, 1892]

We had intended to celebrate our silver wedding but of course will not do so under the circumstances. Rob says, jokingly, he is sorry, for he expected to get away with a barrel or more of silver. We have given away more than that during the years we have lived in Helena on occasions of this kind and this seems our only chance to <u>get even</u>. I don't know but I have all the silver I care to keep in order. . . .

All send love,
L.C. Fisk

Helena, Apr. 11th, 1892

My dear Mother:

Robbie left us quite unexpectedly on Thursday evening last for a hurried trip to Minnesota. Ever since he attended school in Faribault he has corresponded with a young lady in the place, a Miss [Inez] Aldrich. She was considerably older than Robbie, a very nice girl and. . . I think Robbie cared as much for her as it is possible for a boy of his age to care for any one. She wrote him very nice letters and her influence was always for good. . . . Then Inez was taken very ill, the doctors first said pneumonia, then talked of quick consumption, and in March she was so weak as to be unable to see any one or even to speak.

[H]er brother wrote [saying] they were trying a new treatment . . . and she seemed to be gaining, . . . she was sitting up, her cough almost gone and appetite good. For two weeks there was no word, then on Thursday came a telegram "Inez is sinking rapidly. No hope." A later message said "She cannot live thirty-six hours."

But Robbie started that night hoping that knowing he was on the way she might live till he could reach her. . . . I suppose the dear boy needed just this sorrow and discipline to make him a better man, to help develop him "four square," as we heard in the sermon yesterday. . . .

[Apr. 18th, 1892]

You will want to hear of Robbie's journey. He was detained several hours en route and missed his train for Faribault Saturday evening, and on his arrival . . . Sunday morning found the dear girl had been dead two days. So he was only in time to see her laid away. . . . It did seem so hard. . . .

148

[Yesterday] afternoon we attended the furneral of Col. [Charles A.] Broadwater, at least we drove out to the Hotel, and looked on from afar. The crowd was immense, every conveyance in the city was called in requisition and three trains of fifteen cars ran down on the Montana Central to a point near the cemetery. I do not like so much parade on an occasion of this kind, so much publicity given to every word and act of the mourning family. Col. Broadwater's death is a great loss to the community, for he ever had the best interests of the city and state at heart. . . .

With much love.

Your daughter,
L.C. Fisk

The McDermott
A.F. Wey, Proprietor
Butte, Montana
June 13th, 1892

My dear Mother,

As you will surmise we are on our return way from Ogden. I left home on Wednesday . . . in a pouring rain, a terrific thunder shower. . . We found Clarke . . . on the platform in Ogden, took breakfast at the hotel and then drove out to the Academy. Here we witnessed the drill, saw the boys make their beds and put their rooms in order, and strolled about. . . .

Friday morning . . . dawned dark and rainy. The graduating exercises were to take place at two o'clock, and the clouds lifted just long enough to allow the people to come out from town. The commencement was a success, the orations all good and the young men so easy and dignified. . . . [Clarke's] subject . . . was Free Silver, and won many favorable comments from listeners of both political parties. During the closing oration the rain and hail come down in torrents, and the storm continued all the afternoon, till ditches and creeks overflowed, the whole country was flooded, the road to town almost impassable. But many of the young people from town came out to the commencement Ball, the girls of course were lovely and blue coats and brass buttons as irresistible as usual. . . .

We started for home yesterday and should have been in Helena soon after this hour. Washouts are delaying trains and so instead of leaving at 8 A.M. we waited till 3:30. If I reach home tonight I shall be satisfied. The fog and smoke [in Butte] are so thick we cannot see across the streets and the mud, well I know it reaches to shoe top, I cannot tell how much further. . . .

As the day wore away we learned that no train could pass over the Montana Central that day, so Clarke went to the N[orthern] P[acific] agent, told him how we were situated and he gave us passes over his road. We had a great rush to gather up our belongings and reach the depot, but finally left the filthy city about three o'clock. We crossed the main range of the Rockies by the Homestake trail or pass. . . .

We reached Logan on the N.P. road about six o'clock. Bought crackers and cheese, sardines and pickles and lunched in the waiting room. And here we waited till 1:30 A.M. trying to find a soft place on the wooden benches, and resting place for our weary heads, other than a pine board. . . . Then came the . . . whistle and our train appeared. . . . We should have left Logan at 11 and reached Helena about 2 o'clock but it was sunrise when we reached home.

I fell asleep nearly as soon as we started and slept till we were near Helena. At the depot we found neither carriage nor car and had to telephone up town for a conveyance. I do not need to say we were glad to be at home and intend to stay there for the present. . . .

My eyelids are still heavy and it is easy to fall asleep if I sit quietly for a few moments. Will only add much love from all.

Your daughter,
L.C. Fisk

Helena, Sept. 4th, 1892

My dear Mother:

These autumn days are the most beautiful of the whole year. It is a pleasure just to be alive and out of doors. . . .

You [know of] the proceedings in the City Council, the report of the experts and the committee appointed to examine [James Walker's] books. Even if he is able to straighten things out and account for the missing six thousand dollars he has been criminally careless and negligent in his official duties and can never be trusted or respected again. And even now he spends all his time in saloons playing cards for drinks or something else. With all his bright mind his splendid education and great natural abilities, he was wrecked his whole life. And he has a wife and two lovely little boys.

Is there never to be an end to this terrible power of intemperance of whiskey drinking? Those who denounce Prohibition as extreme must be blind to the terrible effects of the use of liquor. . . .

The Andersons have sold their little home on Broadway, also the lots in Grand Avenue Addition. They got in too deep. Mr. A. lost or gave up his position with Wallace and Thornburgh at a salary of $200 per month, times are dull, he is just starting in for himself and had to sell or lose the Lenox house. He disposed of the house and lots advantageously and hopes also to sell the Lenox property. . . .

[Sept. 25th, '92]

Since Rob left I have had a furnace put in the house. Our old stoves were all burnt out and had to be replaced with new ones or newly lined which costs almost as much. We consumed twenty-five cords of wood last winter and then were not comfortable if it was at all cold. So I just made up my mind I had waited long enough and would save dirt and wear on carpets and put my fire in one place instead of four. . . .

[Oct. 9th, 1892]

In putting in the furnace, which is hot air, I had also much to look after. We excavated under the dining room, took out forty-eight cubic yards of earth which made an <u>immense</u> pile which must be hauled away. When the furnace was in I had a carpenter to board up and build a coal bin, put in a window, &c., then a stone mason to plaster up the foundation. Then followed the housecleaning which was not quite completed a week since. . . .

Monday morning

You ask of the medicine. You are to take it right along while it lasts, there were sixty powders so you have enough for a month. The doctor thought if you were feeling pretty well and not flowing you might fancy you did not need the medicine but he wished you to take it regularly. He will send more if you need. . . .

[Oct. 24, 1892]

Please do not destroy my old letters. During one of the last calls [Rev. Francis D.] Kelsey paid us I was indulging in some reminiscences of early days when he said, "You ought to write that down and leave it for your children. It is a matter of history and will be interesting long after you are gone." I told him I had, in letters written to you, a complete story of my life here. He said "take those letters and copy, eliminating whatever you do not wish to make public, and make a book. Do it now, before many things are lost or forgotten."

The suggestion seems a good one. . . . I have always said I should write a book before I died. By weaving in a little romance it might be made quite interesting. . . .

[Nov. 14th, 1892]

On Wednesday . . . news was brought me of the financial troubles
and suspension of the *Journal*. I should be more than human if I did
not rejoice. And I — the family — were not the only ones in Helena
whose hearts were glad. The publication of the paper may be resumed
after a time, if the creditors are able to effect a compromise. Of course
we hope they will not since its suspension means increased prosperity
for the *Herald*. . . .

[Dec. 4th, 1892]

We find the air in our house pure and good. The cold air is supplied
from outside the house, a pipe at least fifteen inches in diameter
bringing in a constant supply which is heated and rises. With the coal
fire it is easy to maintain an almost uniform temperature. A ton of coal
. . . lasted just three weeks. This costs $6.25 so we heat the whole house
three weeks for that amount. We could not have done it with wood. . . .

With much love,
L.C. Fisk

Helena, Feb. 15th, 1893

My dear Mother:

[Yesterday afternoon] we went to the Legislature, to be present at
the joint session when the ballot for U.S. Senator was taken. These wise
lawmakers seem to have as much idea of the honor and dignity of the
positions they hold as a lot of disorderly school boys. Many of them have
come to Helena just to have a good time, "a high old time," I think they
would call it.

More than forty days of the session have passed and they have done
nothing. The two factions of the democracy refuse to unite on a third
candidate whom they might any day elect. Votes have been bought. Mr.
W.A. Clark has spent thousands and Mr. [Marcus] Daly, for his man
[William W.] Dixon, has not been far behind. It is said some of the
Legislators will go home ten thousand dollars richer than when they
came to Helena this winter. . . .

Yesterday afternoon I attended a reception at Mrs. C.W. Cannon's. . . .
In the dressing room as I was coming away there was a tall, fine
looking woman whom I did not know till I heard some one call her Mrs.
Clark — Mrs. J.K. Clark, her husband a brother of W.A. One lady
enquired "How is Cricket?" Mrs. C. replied "Cricket is well but I have
had to leave him alone all day. I attended the wedding this morning,
went out to lunch and came here. I got a girl to come in and stay with
him. Was strongly tempted to bring him here as Mrs. Cannon said it
was wholly informal, &c." I supposed Cricket must be her little boy but
have since learned he is a pet dog. What it is to be "in the swim!" The
fool-killer must have neglected Helena of late. . . .

The last week has been an exciting one, in political circles. We spent a part of two evenings at the Legislature and were also present when the final ballot was taken for U.S. Senator. It was the most exciting scene I ever witnessed. As the roll was called . . . the Senators responded to their names. When [George M.] Hatch, a man whom every one supposed was a staunch Republican, an upright incorruptible man, gave his vote to W.A. Clark, the hall [resounded] with cheers, groans and hisses.

As the roll call proceeded and Dixon Democrats changed their votes to Clark and five other Republicans went back on party pledges, principles and good name and also voted for him, people fairly held their breath till the official count was announced. And still Clark failed to receive the requisite number of votes and no maneuvering on the part of his friends could secure a second ballot.

The immense Auditorium was packed from floor to ceiling. The excitement was intense. Senator [Elmer D.] Matts, a Dixon man, slowly rose and took off his overcoat, and turning, faced the assembled multitude. Then he told his party what he thought of them, of their conduct for nearly sixty days, on any one of which they might have elected a Senator. . . . his face white with suppressed anger.

Then the Populists asserted themselves and they, too, were angry, and when the vote was taken to dissolve the joint session and the gravel fell, the wildest excitement prevailed. The renegade Repulicans were publicly arraigned as traitors and charges of bribery and corruption were freely hurled.

No Senator having been elected, it became necessary for the Governor [John E. Rickards] to appoint and many were the seekers for the position. Col. Sanders was anxious to be his own successor. . . . Tom Carter[1] assured the governor if he was appointed his (the Gov.'s) political future was assured.

But Lee Mantle[2] of Butte was the fortunate man and on Saturday noon his name was given to the people. He is a man of some ability, a self-made man, but a most immoral one. The best women of Butte do not recognize him, so open and notorious are his violations of decency. What combination, sale or bargain led to his appointment has not yet transpired. . . .

I had some poor work . . . during the week, one day Grace and Baby spent with us. . . . The children are all well and busy as can be. Robbie was tired out when the Legislature adjourned, working day and night for the last week.

With much love,
L.C. Fisk

April 18, 1893

Mrs. Azuba Clarke Chester, widow of the late Isaac Chester and mother of Mrs. R.E. Fisk, died at Vernon Center, Conn., at noon to-day, aged 70 years. . . . The expectation was that a month or so hence she would be domiciled in the Helena home and become one of a family of four generations gathered beneath the same roof. But sickness came and the sad announcement of death is now flashed from far away Connecticut. Mrs. Fisk, who had been at her mother's bedside the past several weeks, has the sympathy of family and friends who cannot journey to sustain her in the hour of afflictions. The funeral takes place on Thursday, 20th, at 2 p.m.

Helena Daily Herald

---

[1]Thomas H. Carter, a Republican lawyer, served as Montana's last Territorial Delegate to Congress (1888-1889), its first Representative (1889-1891), and eventually as U.S. Senator (1895-1911).

[2]Lee Mantle edited the Butte *Inter-Mountain*, served as Mayor of the city, and had long been active in Republican politics. The United States Senate refused to seat Mr. Mantle because the Governor, rather than the Legislature, appointed him. As a result, the seat remained vacant until the 1895 Legislative Assembly appointed Thomas Carter.

Fisk Family, 1898. Standing from left, Robbie, Grace, James, Florence; Seated from left, Julia McIntyre Fisk, R.E. Fisk, Stanley, Elizabeth Chester Fisk, Rufus Clarke, Trilby the dog. —Montana Historical Society

Epilog

Please do not destroy my old letters. During one of his last calls Mr. Kelsey . . . said, "You ought to write that down and leave it for your children. It is a matter of history and will be interesting after you are gone." I told him I had, in letters written to you, a complete story of my life here. He said, "take those letters . . . and make a book."

Rev. Francis Kelsey's perceptions of history proved accurate. With her mother's passing, Lizzie's letters home stopped and the modern historian's window on Helena closed. Time transformed Helena from a rowdy gold camp into an urban financial center; and Elizabeth from a Yankee School Ma'am into a stable member of Montana society. She lived another thirty-four years, but her life and that of her family became obscure after 1893, illuminated infrequently in scattered letters, a page from the family Bible, or a photograph.

By 1893, the rigors of newspaper editing began to tell on Robert E. Fisk, fifty-six. He and his forty-seven year old wife looked toward retirement in California, a state they had both visited and enjoyed. December 27, 1902, the *Helena Herald* ended thirty-six years of publication. Robert Fisk sold his business and took part of his family to California where they spent the rest of their lives. Six years to the day after the last issue of the *Herald* appeared on Helena streets, Robert Emmett Fisk died in Berkeley. Elizabeth outlived him by nineteen years, passing away at Berkeley on April 21, 1927.

Grace divorced Hardy Bryan on October 10, 1898. She and her son Stanley continued to live with her parents on Rodney until they moved. Grace remained in Helena, became Society Editor for the *Record-Herald*, and, on April 30, 1903, married Helena dentist, Wall M. Billings. In 1905, Dr. Billings took his family to Berkeley. Sometime after that date, Grace divorced her second husband — they had no children — and thereafter lived in California until her death March 8, 1935, in Los Angeles.

Robbie learned the printer's trade under his father's tutelage at the *Herald*. He moved to the *Record-Herald* after the turn of the century, and ultimately became printshop foreman. In 1901, Robbie married Mamie Yelland. They had no children and finally left Helena in 1917 moving to Lincoln, Montana, where he worked in the forest products industry until his retirement in the 1940's. Mamie died during the early 1920's and was buried near Lincoln. Robbie's cabin on the Blackfoot River served as a summer retreat and reunion spot for the family many years after the bulk of his brothers and sisters left the state. On several occasions Lizzie joined these family vacations. Robert Loveland Fisk died in Lincoln on January 28, 1952, leaving no survivors.

Rufus Clarke married Florence Julia McIntyre in Helena on August 17, 1898. The same year he secured a job as a postal assistant under the supervision of his uncle A.J. Fisk. He continued his employment with the post office until he left Helena to try homesteading in Chouteau County. The effort, and his 1906 attempt to get a post office named "Fisk," proved abortive. He returned to Helena in 1908 and lived with his wife and two children — Clark Chester and Irene Stowell — west of Helena near the Broadwater Hotel. When their home burned in 1921, the family moved to California, where Clarke died May 31, 1938.

Lizzie's third son, Asa Francis, enlisted in the First Montana Volunteers in 1898, and saw duty in the Philippine Islands during 1899 and later. On December 21, 1903, he married Claire Brace Hassler in the Philippines. They had three children. Asa left the service about the time of his marriage and engaged in exporting. He moved to New England in 1914, and died unexpectedly in Beacon Falls, Massachusetts on March 12, 1915.

The twins, Florence Rumley and James Kennett, went with their parents to California in 1902. Florence married Clarence G. White at Berkeley on August 9, 1905, and they had six children. Florence died in Berkeley October 16, 1947. James never married, and, excepting occasional vacations to Montana, lived in the Berkeley area all his life. He passed away in Oakland on September 10, 1951, and among his possessions were his mother's letters, so carefully written and diligently saved. Through the estate of James Fisk, the Montana Historical Society received the Elizabeth Fisk letters in 1952, along with miscellaneous notes and mementoes from various of the children. In 1977, Irene Fisk Blowers, Clarke's daughter, added numerous family photographs to the collection.

Paved highways and jet liners have replaced the *Little Rock* and the bone-jarring stage, linking Montana's capital ever more firmly with the remainder of the nation. Helena itself pushed into and beyond the vacant lots bordering the Fisk property; filled the voids between downtown and Lenox Addition where the Andersons speculated in real estate. Businesses and private homes now clog the "west side" — almost out to the Broadwater Hotel which time and disuse destroyed. Charles Hard's and Auntie Mae's horse ranch also gave way to homes, mobile and otherwise, while urban renewal swept through the business district along Last Chance Gulch like a mining camp fire, leaving a structure standing here and there, spawning vacant lots and phoenix-like modern buildings.

The home Lizzie sought so diligently in the 1860's, cleaned so carefully whenever Robert left town, and remodeled furtively when she could not sell it, stands today at 319 Rodney Street — made over into apartments. Lizzie's letters survive, too. They reflect her faithful correspondence and keen perception. Each contains the information, facts, statistics and peculiarities of the western frontier Lizzie wanted to save. Together they are the book she hoped to write.

James, Asa, Florence, Robbie, Lizzie, Stanley, and their home in Helena, Montana, 1898. —Montana Historical Society

Bibliography

BOOKS

Adams, Paul M., *When Wagon Trails Were Dim*, n.p.: Montana Conference Board of Education of the Methodist Church, 1957.

Allen & Co., *Historical Sketch and Essay on the Resources of Montana; Including a Business Directory of the Metropolis*. Helena: Herald Publishing Co., 1868.

Athearn, Robert G. *Thomas Francis Meagher: An Irish Revolutionary in America*. Boulder: University of Colorado Press, 1949.

Baucus, Jean. *Gold in the Gulch*. Helena: Bar Wineglass Publications, 1981.

_____. *Helena, Her Historic Homes*. Vol. I. Helena: J-G Publications, 1976.

_____. *Helena, Her Historic Homes*. Vol. II. Helena: Bar Wineglass Publications, 1979.

Beal, Merrill D. *I Will Fight No More Forever: Chief Joseph and the Nez Perce War*. Seattle: University of Washington Press, 1963.

Beckwith, C.C. *Ide's Helena City Directory for 1889*. Helena: A.W. Ide, 1889.

Board of Education. *Catalog of Helena Graded Schools*. Helena: n.p., 1879-1893.

Bowen and Co., A.W. *Progressive Men of the State of Montana*. Chicago: A.W. Bowen and Co., circa 1902.

Brown, Mark H. *The Flight of the Nez Perce*. New York: Putnam, 1967.

Burlingame, Merrill S. *The Montana Frontier*. Helena: State Publishing Co., 1942.

Campbell, William C. *From the Quarries of Last Chance Gulch*. 2 vols. Helena: Privately printed, 1951.

Chittenden, Hiram M. *History of Early Steamboat Navigation on the Missouri River*. New York: Francis P. Harper, 1903.

Dowse, Thomas. *The New Northwest, Montana. Helena; Its Past, Present and Future*. Chicago; Commercial Advertiser Co., 1880.

Ege, Robert J. *Tell Baker To Strike Them Hard*. Bellevue, Neb.: Old Army Press, 1970

Graff, James R. *Historic Helena, 1864-1964*. Helena: Home Building and Loan Association, 1964.

Greenfield, M. *The Old Fire Bell on Tower Hill*. Helena: Privately printed, n.d.

Guice, John D.W. *The Rocky Mountain Bench*. New Haven: Yale University Press, 1972.

Heitman, Francis B. *Historical Register and Dictionary of the United States Army*. 2 vols. Washington: GPO, 1903.

Helena Board of Trade. *Helena Illustrated*. Minneapolis: Helena Board of Trade, 1890.

_____. *Reports of the Secretary of the Board of Trade*. 1878-1879, 1887.

Helena Business College. *Catalog*. Helena: Helena Business College, 1884-85.

Ide, A.W. *Helena City Directory for 1888*. Helena: Montana Directory Co., 1888.

Jacobson & Shope, Architects. *Historic Architectural Survey of the Urban Renewal Area for the Urban Renewal Committee of the City of Helena, Montana*. Helena: Urban Renewal Committee, 1968.

Ladies Relief Committee of Helena. *Minutes of Associated Charities*. 1887-91.

Lang, William and Myers, Rex C. *Montana: Our Land and People*. Boulder: Pruett Publishing Company, 1979.

Langford, Nathaniel P. *The Discovery of Yellowstone National Park*. St. Paul: Privately printed, 1905.

Leeson, M.A. *History of Montana, 1739-1885*. Chicago: Warner, Beers and Co., 1885.

Lyman, A.W. *Helena, Montana, Its Past, Present and Future*. Helena: Arthur W. Ide and W.R. Rumsey, n.d.

McKinney, Patricia M. *The First Presbyterian Church in Helena, Montana*. Helena: Thruber's Printing, 1969.

Madsen, Betty M. and Madsen, Brigham D. *North to Montana*. Salt Lake City: University of Utah Press, 1980.

Malone, Michael P. and Roeder, Richard B. *Montana As It Was: 1876*. Bozeman: Endowment and Research Foundation, Montana State University, 1976.

_____. *Montana: A History of Two Centuries*. Seattle: University of Washington Press, 1976.

Miller, D. Allen. *Helena City Directory*. Helena: George E. Boos, 1886.

Miller, Joaquin. *An Illustrated History of the State of Montana*. Chicago: The Lewis Publishing Co., 1894.

Montana Historical Society. *Not in Precious Metals Alone, a Manuscript History of Montana*. Bozeman: Montana Historical Society, 1976.

Montana Legislative Assembly. *Compiled Statutes of Montana*. Helena: Journal Publishing Co., 1888.

Moore, T.V. *History of the First Presbyterian Church of Helena, Montana.* Helena: Privately printed, n.d.

Myers, Rex C. *Montana's Trolleys.* Book 1, *Helena.* South Gate, Calif.: Ira L. Swett, 1970

Owings, Ralph E. *Montana Directory of Public Affairs, 1864-1960.* Ann Arbor: Privately printed, 1960.

Petrik, Paula. *No Step Backward: Women and Family on the Rocky Mountain Mining Frontier, Helena, Montana, 1865-1900.* Helena: Montana Historical Society Press, 1987.

Polk and Co., R.R. *Helena City Directory.* Vol. I-XIII. Helena: R.L. Polk and Co., 1890-1902

Spence, Clark C. *Territorial Politics and Government in Montana, 1864-1889.* Illinois: University of Chicago Press, 1975.

Staring, George B. *Helena Directory, 1883-84.* Helena: George E. Boos and Co., 1884.

Steele and Co. *Montana Advertising Directory, 1883-84.* Helena: George E. Boos and Co., 1884.

Toole, K. Ross. *Montana: An Uncommon Land.* Norman: Univeristy of Oklahoma Press, 1959.

Tuttle, Daniel S. *Reminiscences of a Missionary Bishop.* New York: Thomas Whittaker, 1906.

United States Geological Survey. *Metaliferous Deposits of the Greater Helena Mining Region.* Bulletin 842. Washington: GPO, 1933.

Waldron, Ellis L. *Montana Politics Since 1864.* Missoula: Montana State University Press, 1958.

Walker, James Blaine. *A Boy Pioneer in the West and Other Reminiscences.* n.p., circa 1963.

Wallace, Robert C. *A Few Memories of a Long Life.* Helena: Privately printed, n.d.

Warner, F.W. *Montana Territory, History and Business Directory, 1879.* Helena: Fisk Brothers, 1879

White, Helen M. (ed.) *Ho! For the Gold Fields.* St. Paul: Minnesota Historical Society, 1966.

Work Projects Adminstration, Mineral Resources Survey. *Bibliography of the Geology and Mineral Resources of Montana.* Montana Bureau of Mines and Geology, Memoir No. 21. Butte: Montana School of Mines, 1942.

ARTICLES

Athearn, Robert G. "Railroad to a Far-Off Country: The Utah and Northern." *Montana, the Magazine of Western History* XVII, r (Autumn, 1968).

Bayne, Nedra. "The Broadwater: Relic of Elegance." *Montana, the Magazine of Western History* XIX, 3 (Summer, 1969).

Brown, Mark. H. "Yellowstone Tourists and the Nez Perce." *Montana, the Magazine of Western History* XVI, 3 (Summer, 1966).

Davison, Stanley R. "1871: Montana's Year of Political Fusion." *Montana, the Magazine of Western History* XXI, 2 (Spring, 1971).

Davison, Stanley R. and Tash, Dale. "Confederate Backwash in Montana Territory." *Montana, the Magazine of Western History* XVII, 4 (Autumn, 1967).

Fletcher, Robert. "Last Chance Gulch." *Montana, The Magazine of Western History* III, 4 (Autumn, 1953).

Hedges, Cornelius. "Historical Sketch of Lewis and Clark County, Montana, July 4, 1876." *Contributions of the Historical Society of Montana* II (1896).

"Helena, the Capital of Montana." *The Northwest Magazine* IV, 7 (July, 1886).

Jackson, W. Turrentine. "The Washburn-Doane Expedition into the Upper Yellowstone, 1870." *The Pacific Historical Review* X, 2 (June, 1941).

Johnson, Dorothy M. "Some Exciting Years in the Past of Montana's Capital City as Seen Through Teen-Age Eyes." *Montana, the Magazine of Western History* XII, 1 (Winter, 1962).

Myers, Rex C. "The Fateful Numbers, 3-7-77: A Re-examination." *Montana, the Magazine of Western History* XXIV, 4 (Autumn, 1974).

_____. "The Montana Club, Symbol of Elegance." *Montana, the Magazine of Western History* XXVI, 4 (Autumn, 1976).

_____(ed.) "To The Dear Ones At Home: Elizabeth Fisk's Missouri River Trip, 1867." *Montana, the Magazine of Western History*, XXXII, 3 (Summer, 1982).

Peterson, Robert L. "The Completion of the Northern Pacific Railroad System in Montana: 1883-1893." In Michael P. Malone and Richard B. Roeder (eds.), *The Montana Past An Anthology.* Missoula: University of Montana Press, 1969.

Petrik, Paula. "Mothers and Daughters of Eldorado: The Fisk Family of Helena, M.T., 1867-1902." *Montana, The Magazine of Western History*, XXXII, 3 (Summer, 1982).

Robison, Willard B. "Helena's Fabulous Business Blocks." *Montana, the Magazine of Western History*, XVIII, 1 (Winter, 1968).

Schreiner, M. Murray. "Last Chance Gulch Becomes the Mountain City of Helena." *Montana, the Magazine of Western History*, II, 4 (Autumn, 1952).

Silliman, Lee. "The Carroll Trail: Utopian Enterprise." *Montana, Magazine of Western History* XXIV, 2 (Spring, 1974).

Smalley, E.V. "The New State of Montana and Its Capital City." *The Northwest Magazine* VIII, 6 (June, 1890).

Spence, Clark C., "Spoilsman in Montana: James M. Ashley." *Montana, the Magzine of Western History* XVIII, 2 (Spring, 1968).

Stanley, Edwin J. "A Brief History of the M.E. Church, South, in Montana from 1864 to 1884." *Minutes of the Seventh Session of The Montana Annual Conference, Methodist Episcopal Church, South.* Kansas City: Ramsey, Millett and Hudson, 1884.

Thane, James L., Jr. "The Myth of Confederate Sentiment in Montana." *Montana, the Magazine of Western History*, XVII, 2 (Spring, 1967).

NEWSPAPERS

Helena Herald. 1866-1902.　　　*Helena Independent.* 1874-1893.

Helena Journal. 1889-1892.　　　*Helena Record.* 1888-1889.

Townsend Tranchant. 1884-1890.

UNPUBLISHED MATERIALS

Albright, R.E. "The Relations of Montana with the Federal Government, 1864-89. Ph.D. dissertation, Stanford University, Stanford, 1933.

Brown, Firman M., Jr. "A History of the Theater in Montana." Ph.D. dissertation, University of Wisonsin, Madison, 1963.

Fisk Family Geneology, Archives/Manuscript Division, Minnesota Historical Society, St. Paul.

Hakola, John W. "Samuel T. Hauser and the Economic Development of Montana." Ph.D. dissertation, Indiana Unviersity, Bloomington, 1961.

Hartman, Bernard Lyle. "A History of Helena's Public Elementary Schools." M. Ed. thesis, Montana State University, Bozeman, 1968.

Holter, Anton M. "History of Anton M. Holter." Typescript, Montana Historical Society.

Lubick, George M. "Cornelius Hedges: The Montana Years, 1864-1907." Ph.D. dissertation, University of Toledo, Toledo, 1974.

Myers, Rex C. "History of the Street Railways in Helena, Montana, 1883-1928." M.A. thesis, University of Montana, Missoula, 1969.

Olson, Rolf Y. "The Nez Perce, the Montana Press, and the War of 1877." M.A. thesis, University of Montana, Missoula, 1974.

Rafferty, Robert O. "The History and Theory of Capital Punishment in Montana." M.A. thesis, Univeristy of Montana, Missoula, 1968.

U.S. Bureau of the Census. Lewis and Clark County, Manuscript Census Returns, 1870.

——————. Lewis and Clark County, Manuscript Census Returns,1880.

White, Thomas Edward. "Cornelius Hedges: Uncommon Hero of Common Life." M.A. thesis, Montana State University, Bozeman, 1963.

165

Andrew Jackson Fisk:
Incoming Corresp., 1861-1865.
Diaries, 1864-1896
Scrapbooks, 3 vols, n.d.

Asa J. Fisk:
Outgoing Corresp., 1886-1901.

Elizabeth Chester Fisk:
Incoming Corresp.,, 1864-1909.
Outgoing Corresp., 1867-1893.
Sketches, 1867

Florence Fisk:
Outgoing Corresp., 1889-1891.

Grace C. Fisk:
Outgoing Corresp., 1875-1888.

James Fisk:
Outgoing Corresp., 1891.

Robert Emmett Fisk:
Incoming Corresp., 1861-1901.
Outgoing Corresp., 1859-1892.

Robert L. Fisk:
Incoming Corresp., 1881.
Outgoing Corresp., 1886.

Azuba Clark Chester:
Incoming Corresp., 1870-1871.

Index

alcohol, 40, 44, 46, 52, 65, 80,
  123-124, 125, 127, 132, 134, 145
Anaconda, 115
Anderson, Clifford, 111, 121, 150
Ashley, James M., 63, 66, 69

Baker, Eugene, 68, 69, 80
Baronett, John, 62
Baxter, B.R., 52
Beall, Samuel W., 54
bed bug, 51, 73
Beem, Martin, 34
Big Hole Battle, 101
Billings, Wall M., 157
Bitterroot, 121
Blaine, John E., 91, 131
Bohm, S.H., 40, 78
Boulder City, 120-121
boxing, 53
Bozeman, 69
Broadwater Hotel, 115, 135, 136,
  149
Broadwater, Charles A., 144, 149
Bryan, Charles Stanley, 116
Bryan, George Hardy, 115-116,
  137, 139, 145, 157
Bullard, William M., 30, 40, 70
burglary, 129-130

Callaway, James E., 84, 94
Camp Baker, 105
Cannon, C.W., 152

capital election, 84, 114-115
capital, 94
Carleton, 111
Carter, Maggie 124
Carter, Thomas H., 114
Catholic, 78, 128
Cavanaugh, James M., 35
Centennial Exposition, 87, 98
Chemidlin, T.N., 40
Chester, Azuba Clarke, 8, 144-
  146, 154
Chester, Fannie, 63, 76
Chester, Isaac, 8, 144, 146
Child, William C., 91
Chinese, 83, 91
Chumasero, Miss, 71
Clagett, William H., 74
Clark, A.G., 15
Clark, J.K. Mrs., 152
Clark, William A., 114, 130, 152,
  153
Coliseum Theatre, 136
Collins, Timothy E., 94
Comfort, George, 52-53
Compton, Arthur L., 61
Compton, Joseph Wilson, 61
Congregational, 147
Corinne, Utah, 73, 87
Council Bluffs, 17
Cruse, Thomas, 115, 124
Curtin, J.C., 128
Curtis, J.D., 128

167

169